27 November 2019

To Céline,

An honour to meet you!
And thank you for reading my poem

The MINISTRY of DREAMS

in the Presentation School,

With every good wish,

Michael Murphy

With affection I dedicate this book to my dear friends, Fiona Coffey and Margaret Martin, to acknowledge their unwavering support and guidance.

MICHAEL MURPHY

The MINISTRY of DREAMS

COLLECTED POEMS

This collection first published by Toga Books in 2019
Dublin, Ireland
www.michaelmurphyauthor.com
Republic of Love first published by Liberties Press, 2013
A Chaplet of Roses first published by Toga Books, 2015

Copyright © 2019 Michael Murphy

Paperback	ISBN: 978-1-78846-107-8
Ebook – mobi format	ISBN: 978-1-78846-108-5
Ebook – ePub format	ISBN: 978-1-78846-109-2
Amazon paperback	ISBN: 978-1-78846-110-8

All rights reserved. No part of this book may be reproduced or utilised in any form or by any means electronic or mechanical, including photocopying, filming, recording, video recording, photography, or by any information storage and retrieval system, nor shall by way of trade or otherwise be lent, resold or otherwise circulated in any form of binding or cover other than that in which it is published without prior permission in writing from the author.

The right of Michael Murphy to be identified as the author of the work has been asserted by him in accordance with the Copyright, Designs and Patents Act 1988.

A CIP catalogue record for this book is
available from the British Library

Produced by Kazoo Independent Publishing Services
222 Beech Park, Lucan, Co. Dublin
www.kazoopublishing.com

Kazoo Independent Publishing Services is not the publisher of this work. All rights and responsibilities pertaining to this work remain with Toga Books.

Kazoo offers independent authors a full range of publishing services.
For further details visit www.kazoopublishing.com

Illustrations and cover image by Colin Eaton
Back Cover photograph by José Luis Veiga
Cover design by Andrew Brown
Printed in the EU

Contents

Introduction   xi

Republic of Love

Flowers

The Poppy	19
The Daffodil	20
The Sunflower	21

Spain

Spain	25
The Pilgrim	26
Nöeleen	28
La Dama de Noche	30
Season's Change	31
A Lost Christmas	32
La Concha	33
Tarifa	34

Sexuality

An Ode to Those Labelled "Intrinsically Disordered"	39
The People of the Book	40

Emotions

A Dignified Silence	45
On Contemplation	46
Fear	48

Radio

Radio Four	53
Here Is the News	54
Eau De	57

Love

To Those Who Have Given Up on Love	61
Auburn – For Mary	65
Celibate Men in Dresses	66
Gloria in Excelsis	69
Benedicite – for Jeanne and Mark	70
Epithalamion: A Poem for Terry	72

A Chaplet of Roses

Introduction	81

Flora and Fauna

And When You Speak of Trees	85
Anna's Dog Toga	87
Bad Behaviour Can Get Elephants Killed	89

Poems for Friends

Seven	93
My Perfect Ruby	96

On Food

Bread	101
Figs and Blue Cheese	103
The Kiwi	104

On Death and Dying

I Shall Die	107
Enough	108
Interruption	110
Hail and Farewell	111
Relationships Do Not Die	113

Some Personal Poems

The Seeker	117
On Turning Sixty-five	119
Bereft	120
Belfast	121
Complicity	122
Email to ISIS	123
Repetition	126
Devotion	127

The Mayo Sequence

Home to Mayo	131
A Vote for Love	135
A Chaplet of Roses	139

The Ministry of Dreams

Introduction	147

Toga the Chocolate Labrador

My Dog and the Meaning of Life	151
And I Am Truly Blessed	152

Love Poems

A Poem for Terry	159
Loss	161
Elysium	163
How I Could Help You	164

Politics

Madam President	169
Email to Donald Trump	171
A New Republic	173

Personal Poems

Misericord	177
Queen of the May	179
Christmas	181
Poet in His Home Town	182
Terry's Mother Sarah	190
Heretic	191
Lorca with Whitman's Butterflies	193
Joni Mitchell's 75th Birthday Tribute	195
My Father's Language	197
On Writing	199
Gaudete	201
Full Speech	202
A Life for Love	204
Polio and Growing Older	207

Poems for Friends

Brothers	213
And We Shall Be a Blessing	217
Eternally Yours	219
Love that Is Always Here	223

His Royal Highness	226
The Madrid Journalist	228
My Own Woman	229
I Am the Minister of Children Who Dream	233
Original Forewords and Postface	247
Acknowledgements	278

Gentle reader,

These poems are for your reading and listening pleasure. So dip into this collection at random and find some words that speak to you of love or hope and offer encouragement for living.

This Collected Poems is made up of three books. *The Republic of Love* and *A Chaplet of Roses* were published in 2013 and 2015, and the new poems in *The Ministry of Dreams* appear here for the first time, published in 2019.

The Republic of Love title comes from the poem I wrote as a wedding gift for my life partner Terry on the occasion of our Civil Partnership:

"Side by side we laid our bouquet of roses out at the GPO
Acknowledged those who gave their lives so we could be cherished equally
Proclaimed ourselves free and free to become
Better together than either of us could choose to achieve on our own
And we withdrew relevance from those who disapproved
Of our new and mutual republic of love …"

This initial collection features *The Poppy* poem, written after surviving cancer, and which sets the tone for the book:
"… how glorious a thing it is
To be alive and laughing in the wind
Extravagantly scattering my seeds of happiness and hope
And being wild and flagrant and dancing
Like a single red poppy in a whole field of yellowing corn"

In the poem *To Those Who Have Given Up On Love* there's the warmest invitation to "Wear the clothes of the love story of your life…" It's my earnest wish as you whisper aloud these poetic words of wonder.

Enjoy the music,

MICHAEL MURPHY

And for today's eternity how glorious a thing it is
To be alive and laughing in the wind
Extravagantly scattering my seeds of happiness and hope
And being wild and flagrant and dancing
Like a single red poppy in a whole field of yellowing corn

THE POPPY

The Republic of Love

A Note from the Artist

I ENJOY ABSTRACTION OF TYPE, indeed abstraction of form, which probably comes from my architectural training of taking into account givens: the site and context and moulding shapes and planes to create space. Given the vividness of the red of poppies and the yellowness of a field of corn, I thought that would be enough. So the form is abstracted. Lots of verticals become the sheaves of corn, and the poppy stands proud within that.

COLIN EATON.

Flowers

The Poppy

Because there is no point to anything anyway
It is necessary to be defiant and protesting
Like a single red poppy in a field of yellowing corn

And because I care so desperately that there is no point
I keenly feel the deadly sadness underlying it all

I know there is no voice that is like unto mine
There never was
Nor will there ever be again
For my time under the warmth of the sun
Which will set

And so there is no reason never to be
Outrageous or resplendent as a poppy
Bright red erect and generously
Giving difference to the sameness of that field of corn
Shouting out that I was born for better or for worse
Waving my flag and making my colourful noise
And frightening away the darkness for as long as possible

To become the best poppy that ever there was
Is no mean ambition because it means
To take on the responsibility of caring for myself
And not to lean on or to take from others' kindnesses

And for today's eternity how glorious a thing it is
To be alive and laughing in the wind
Extravagantly scattering my seeds of happiness and hope
And being wild and flagrant and dancing
Like a single red poppy in a whole field of yellowing corn

The Daffodil

I desire to be as free as the daffodil
For daffodils dance in the wind and the rain
Like children at play laughing and waving
Celebrating in the green spring

Those brilliant yellow Lent lilies
Are risen from the dead after suffering underground
And offer the promise of a resurrection
Nodding their assent to the dream of the impossible

Their glance is more tenuous from having survived the past
Fearless of tomorrow they live only for today
And give prodigally blooming in profusion
Delighting the soul with yellow brightness
Inviting me courageously onwards towards the summer
Illuminating steps with lighted lanterns

So changed from having lost
Aware of limits lacking that much more
I embrace the cost of a new life
A second time around

Another chance to flame with love
The last dance better than before
I have endured like the daffodil
I too am above ground
And mostly I am childishly grateful

The Sunflower

The sunflower stares at the sun
It is held in a mutual gaze like a baby
Cradled in the bower of an arm
I place you at the centre of my life
To comfort you whenever you need me
I vow to keep you free from harm
Eternally

Underneath a cloudless sky
The summer heat lies heavy
On the fields of yellow sunflowers
That surround my whitewashed house in Spain
Protecting it like an army of smiling soldiers

From the brow of a hill thrust up into the blue
I survey the open faces of the troops
Marshalled in peaceful rows like Roman legionaries
Worshipping Mithras the god of searing light
Long ago in timeless Iberia

Spain

Spain

The flaring light of Spain
Powders the air
With a dusting of white gold
Accumulating on the horizon
Leaching blue from the sky
A layering centuries old

The heightened light of Spain
Brimmed at my eyes
Like golden olive oil
And overflowed into my soul
Dripping unceasingly

The Pilgrim

It may be Guidera
That forebear of my great-grandmother
Set sail aboard a galleon
From Galicia

My father's sister Aunt Isabella remembered visiting
Two Guidera women
In the twenties
In Borris-in-Ossory
And my father always said his father
Had a sallow complexion like a Spaniard
We have the photograph to prove it
A Laois *campesino*
Rich with Guidera blood

Tradition in the family says Guidera was a guide
who survived the Spanish Armada
Like St James *Matamoros*
Cast ashore and cut adrift
What did he feel
When first he saw the coast of Ireland
To misapprehend the green like Galicia under the sun
For what was cold and unwelcoming as winter
What sort of map did Guidera have
That he should negotiate a shipwreck
In of all places Borris-in-Ossory

Was he inured to harshness
Did he experience tenderness
Charging the loins fuelling Irish lust
Some seventeen-year-old

with sallow skin and agile body
Exotic as Spanish olive oil

Did they share a faith in common – this is my body –
Was their pleasure all the sweeter for Catholic guilt
He traded her a name against another son for Spain
His children exiles in their own land
But she gave him place

Nevertheless the mystery remains
What compass guided Guidera
And did he return to Spain
To reclaim his heritage

Or did his son become the pilgrim
Or was I the one to undertake
the Camino de Santiago
And bring his relics home

Nöeleen

What do you do
When a woman gives you the gift of herself
How do you repay that

When she enfolds your hand in hers
And looks through your eyes
In an instant entrusting herself to what she sees there
What can you say in return

I know a woman in Spain
Born at the time of the Christ child
Who takes the weft of God
And tries unendingly
To weave the threads of man through it
So that now you are always at the centre
And never at life's edge

How do I make amends
Or do I do you a disservice
By not responding in a new way
Do you see the little boy
And know the meaning of the joy
that each new day's dawning brings for him

You cut him free from the prism of ice that skews his light
By calling up the man
"Relax – it'll be alright – you're at your granny's"

Now that I am here in focus
What do you want of me

Nothing
Utter indifference
I be me in my way
You be you in yours
And from the tension of the opposites
We create together the Godhead
A new word yet to be spoken on earth
So that I can continue
To weave my thread through
Haven't you heard it yet

I need you for this
That is why I never stand in any man's light
She gently polished my forehead with a kiss
"Shine" she whispered
"Shine" I said
And I switched on
The universe

La Dama de Noche

La Dama de Noche her perfume
Visited me in my room
She suffused me with scent
Tried to seduce me with blandishments
"You know" she said, "that Spain has set a table
Just for you under the sun"
It was natural not to yield to question "Why? Why me?"
While this simple extravagance of La Dama's gift
Required the response "Why not?"

She was insistent that place-setting was mine
"It's in your name" she said "If you don't fill it then who will?"
The initial choice it seems was made by Spain
In the ninth month of ninety-nine I was born a child of light
Dare I disturb the universe and make that choice my own?
If I refuse it will be as if I never had been
Withering without taking root
If I assent then all I had been I will lose

I desire to take my place
To flower in daylight
Scenting the air with my presence
I desire to espouse La Dama de Noche
And become a powerful man in the bounteous banquet of life
Under the nurturing sun of Spain
So that I in my turn can give light
And become in my turn
A courageous son
Of Spain

Season's Change

Autumn arrived early this morning
So unexpectedly in Elviria

I surfaced from a dreamless sleep shrouded in sweat
And blundered to the bathroom to piss and wet the floor tiles

The leaves of the *palmeras* barked in the sudden levanter
Souls that got lost in their solitude out past Tarifa
Saw me inside and rattled their bones
Begging for the love of Allah
I had to close the window on their terror

When I awoke the whole area was being painted
With wraiths of cold mist which dimmed the lustre
Savaging the sunlight writing shape-shifting cuneiform
Characters telling me that autumn had arrived

In a shiver of circling black and white storks
Hundreds of them turning around overhead
Streaming south in the thermals
Drawing ghosts in their wake

I thought I heard or read a despairing scream in autumn's echo
Just before the sun burnt up the tale of the damned
In the blazing searing heat of the Costa del Sol summer

A Lost Christmas

We lost Christmas on the Costa del Sol
The windy coast it was closed "No peoples …"
An English couple hanging onto Santa hats
And bottle trophies from a garage supermarket
Supported one another

At lunch alone we looked
And silently fleeing Bing Crosby's "White Christmas"
Stammering tips in the pizzeria in Elviria
Escaped to where?
Feliz navidad!

La Concha

Red is the colour of Marbella's mountain
Scrawled in God's fresh blood beneath the blue-veined sky
An outing covenant danced in black
With clacking heels across this tract of plain
The flourish of a final turn reveals
A red-emblazoned serpent shimmering

Red is the colour of God's signature
Slumbering under a clear blue sky
A red mountain mantra inscribed across
The talisman of a reflecting frieze
Evoking the latent voice of God
A ruby-red rioja from the juice of blackened grapes

Red is the *muleta* trailed by God across the sand
A red flamenco frock swirling like the wild levanter
Plunging to the hilt to the heart the sword
A roaring gush of vivid red unfurling
Cruel as the reddest sun that rises suddenly
Searing those stamping footsteps into the black bull's skin

Red is the colour of Marbella's mountain
Kohled black eyes shaded beneath mantilla grilles
The far-off gaze of God is straight and proud unwavering
A red paper flower flies to earth from out of this dancer's hair
And is kicked to the side in a flounce of strutting skirts
It creates the red arena for the inevitable ending
Of a final dance with God a dance with death

Tarifa

The wind always blows on the beach at Tarifa
Sweeping along the sand folding and unfolding
Whipping up the grains into the sizzling air
And tossing them about like the kite-flyer angels
With colourful wings skimming across the breaking waves
Fallen angels sand-blasted black against the scorching sun
Polished by unbearable light stepping out of the sea
In a glittering cloud of glory embodying
The same unchanging message for mankind
The wind always blows on the beach at Tarifa

God walks in the wind on that beach at Tarifa
He presses his lips to the shore in a kiss
And leaves his spittle frothing on the sand
He whistles through the pines by the drifting dunes
He write his name writhing like a snake
And when he turns the locals say that meat goes bad
His gaze is ferocious screaming out of the storm
Burning my soul with his psychotic certainties
The wind always blows on the beach at Tarifa

I contended with my God on that beach at Tarifa
We leaped together into the turbulent air
Holding hands like lovers ascending
Wheeling around exulting up into the blue
I held his implacable gaze against the sun
And I reproached him for life having happened to me
He plundered the complaint from my mouth with the wind
But I listened to my lamentation moaning desolately in the trees
As we soared towards an acceptance of what is
and I refused it as not being good enough
I withheld compliance from the inevitable ending

Of just another grain of sand being scattered by the breeze
For the wind always blows on the beach at Tarifa

I dared to dream I chose to shine
Like the evanescent morning star
Or to behave like the brightest shooting star falling from heaven
I am my own man I said and thought of Lucifer and Luther
I courageously claimed freedom for even the shortest arc of time
Knowing that my glorious revolt precedes a restoration
For the wind always blows on that beach at Tarifa

Sexuality

An Ode to Those Labelled "Intrinsically Disordered"

We remember the terror of the men and of the women
Who are still denounced
Once they were burned at the stake
Their lives extinguished at Buchenwald
Who are still in prison

To have a legal way of being
Powerless
Because they happen to be homosexual

I owe them so much honour

The People of the Book

The People of the Book
Condemn me for being
A person who loves
Those of my own sex

The Christians the Muslims
And even the Jews
(Who attest to the lack of redemption)
Believe that God says
For me to be loving
I'd have to be living in sin

The Nazis decided I'm *untermensch*
A subhuman person
To be burned in the ovens at Buchenwald
The German Pope
Following on in that tradition
Decreed that as a human being
I'm "intrinsically disordered …
with a tendency towards evil"
A ranking so far beneath
That of the heterosexual elect
I'm destined to be burned in the fires of hell
For all eternity

The People of the Book
See nothing wrong with that prejudice
They consider themselves nice people
"If it were up to them …" But it's not
God is the despot here

The People of the Book believe
I have a dialect of sexuality
Which must be suppressed
For the sake of the family
Or because the "grotesquery" of gay marriage
Poses "the biggest threat to our civilisation"
Bigger even than global warming
(I recall from those harrowing documentaries on television
The same threat was once laid at the door of the Jews)
Do the People of the Book hope that the millions of us
Will be obliterated off the face of the earth?
Or should we voluntarily submit ourselves to castration by dogma
For differing sexually from the majority?

The People of the Book
Ignore the advances in human psychology
Which say that my dialect of sex
Is a normal outcome of the Oedipus complex
They say they take their instruction
From Moses and Jesus and Muhammad
Whom they preach with all the fanatical certainty
Of the ignorant and insecure

The People of the Book suggest
That I should press my sexuality
Between the leaves of the good book
So that it can wither away like a desiccated flower
For according to them my "out" sexuality
Is not orthodox not sanctioned
By people who monopolise the deity

The tragedy for me
Is that the People of the Book
Would exclude me from a sense of the sacred
Which I find in the wonder of love

And in the various expressions of human nature

I can hear God speak through the human voice
That tells me I'm alright despite my differences
That encourages me to continue on when times get tough
Helping me to hope for better
That is humble enough to walk beside me on the road
On every journey of my life
That makes a commitment to a fellow human being
Reaching out to lift the heavy burden off my shoulders
That trusts me unconditionally with the courage
To live out my truth in spite of doubt
Responsible only to the best that I can be
Flowering in my own way at my own pace
Without feeling the need to berate me as the scapegoat
The outsider the stranger
The prodigal son the neighbour

That can always say to me the Jew
Me the Christian me the Muslim
Me the son of God
"I believe in you
Because I love you"

And also (a dialect the People of the Book conveniently forget)
"Because you are mine" says the Lord

Emotions

A Dignified Silence

Against a three-year-old child
Being beaten to within an inch of his life
We have maintained a dignified silence

Against a seven-year-old child
Being sexually molested by several men
We have maintained a dignified silence

Against a teenager
Coping with the strain of an alcoholic father
We have maintained a dignified silence

Against a gay twenty-year-old
Daring to come out to an unaccepting world
We have maintained a dignified silence

Against my brother wasting away from cancer
Living out of love as long as possible
We have maintained a dignified silence

Against myself attacked by prostate cancer
Without continence still impotent
We have maintained a dignified silence

And for you my brother we would have wished the same
Not to speak about the horror nor to have had your say
But to take your stand with us in maintaining to the last
A dignified silence

On Contemplation

Here in this *terra incognita*
I vanquish with Apollo
What is familiar to me from before
The insular ghostly grey sea-mist

In a ritual morning battle
The deadening gloom is put to flight
And the blinding light
Shines in triumph all the day long
From skies the colour of lapis lazuli

I hear the clicking afternoon heat
Lie heavy as a bed sheet
Cast aside from the boiling vastness
Of this rumpled lurid land

I cry out at the sight
Of lemons fallen from trees

I turn towards the sweetly fragrant jasmine
Wafting in the breeze

I take delight in rough hewn walls
Imprinting whitewash on my hands
These Cubist surrounds of Andalus pueblos

In further exploring the newness
I taste the golden fruit of the sun
Pressed oil from olives locally grown

I am describing here contemplation
A mode of being where my voice soars
Across the face of heaven with the sun

From this vantage point
I can look back at those I left behind
And measure how far I have come

Recall all the pioneering lands
Through which I passed to reach here
And find treasure

Fear

I feel afraid all the time
Fear is my default setting
I grin and greet people
Inside I feel terrified

At the end of a pier in the dark
I fold my clothes in a bundle
I leave my car keys in my shoes
And slip silently over the edge
Drowning in a winter sea

What toppled the terror over?
Too weighty suddenly
A flight into the lapping blackness
So that I continue to fall forever
Frozen with fear

Don't hand on the shock to others
"If only we had known
We would have done something …"
I have always known
There was nothing I could have done differently

I have excavated the truth
Excoriated it with words
So that it was stripped bare
To the bone

The skeletal face of a drowning man
The rigid open mouth
No resources left
No protective skin

The unavailing barrier of a hollow grin

To much suffocating truth

Radio

Radio Four

I want to live in Radio Four
Where the accents are creamily redolent
Of cotswold stone

Where I overheard the writer Joanna Trollope say
"I once had a friend who revived a panicked sheep
with an entire bottle of rescue remedy"

Guests paint a picture with proper words
Pronounced with care

I long to live there

Here Is the News

The announcer came on at six o'clock in the morning
She wished us all "Happy Gnu Year!"
And said "Over now to Michael Murphy in the Gnu's room …"

For a second I was struck dumb
Affronted
Then I recovered myself

A gnu (pronounced noo) is an antelope
Which inhabits the savannahs of Africa
I've seen it on television
It has an ox-like head and a long tufted tail

I know a gnu was a mythical beast as well
Believed to live along the banks of the river Euphrates
But "Happy Gnu Year" made no sense to me

"Over now to Michael Murphy in the Gnu's room"
Sounded denigrating perhaps a comment
On the supposed wildebeest habits of my newsroom colleagues

I could never begin a bulletin with "Here is the gnus"
Because the sentence is grammatically incorrect
It should read "Here are the gnus" by way of introducing
The herd of springbok and impala
The blackbuck and dikdik
That would suddenly proliferate inexplicably in a news script

In my forty years as a broadcaster I've never had to do that
"Here is the news" yes "Here are the gnus" no
So when I hear the announcer go "Happy Gnu Year"

I want to become a hunter like Ernest Hemingway
And yes I want to kill but not a helpless animal
Rather somebody who should have known better
Than to take me unawares
And profane my writer's ear at six o'clock in the morning

I question whether a radio station
Grounded as it is in the spoken word
Can be taken seriously
If it doesn't make an effort to sound intelligent

We are all bound to find ourselves in language
A common property that we turn into a personal tool to communicate
What impression did our Taoiseach make on foreign heads of state
When he mangled his syntax?
Was he saved by the skills of the translator?
How can today's poets write poetry?
It's not possible if they don't know that constable rhymes with cup
Or that precedent turns into a cupboard and becomes un-press-edented
When one puts an un in front of it

A writer or speaker implies
What a reader or hearer infers
So that somebody talking about an antelope at six o'clock in the
    morning
Leads me to reason since I am enfolded into that broadcast
That I'm being wished a happy year as a bovid or as a mammal

But if a presentation announcer was parading
Her basic ignorance of English speech
By invoking a procession of graceful gazelle
When her intention was merely to send out a greeting
And simply to wish us well in the coming year
What hope is there of legal safety from uncaring savages
Even if we seek justice in a thicket of linguistic difference and truth?

What hope is there of relating openly to my fellow-man my brother
And being nourished by his care and by his love
If one word can sound and mean the same
As any Annie other udder?

Eau De

I closed the microphone
And slowly released with relief
A pent-up plosive reverberating very early morning fart
Into the close confines
Of the tiny news heads' studio

The enveloping odour was of old wet dog
With intimate notes of decaying dead rat
Trapped beneath the floorboards
So poisonously acrid
"It'd take the brand off a sack" as my late father used to say
Way beyond any ineffectual dispersal
Through waving a news script at the fumes
From behind the chair

When I opened the microphone again
The door burst open
And in walked Pauric Lodge
To read the sports news

The revised Christmas schedule contains
Many such rich surprises

I hadn't the heart to chide him
For the overpowering stench
Of his expensive eau de toilette
Which filled the studio with
A very welcome Christmas gift

We sat opposite each other
In a warm but impregnable silence
Preparing our scripts for the broadcast
Each of us almost afraid to breathe

Love

To Those Who Have Given Up on Love

To those who have given up on love
I reach out my hand
Shivering at the depth of your personal despair
I shut my mouth on intrusive questions
Is it because you feel unworthy
Or has life unfairly passed you by

Here is a hand you can hold onto
For a while
For whatever reason
If that is what you want
Although I know it's not
Enough
Until you find your footing once again
And you will
Inevitably
Fall
And recover slower
And with less resilience
As you grow
Older

Put your hand in mine
And let the warmth of my embrace
Begin to thaw the neglect that you have lived with
Withering away from winter's harsh unfeeling winds
Smiling mysteriously to conceal a broken heart
Your embarrassing pain
Too apparent to everyone
As out of place here

As the suppurating wound of your grief

I can see that others have hurt you
You've suffered from the cruelty of carelessness
From the thoughtless exuberance of youth
From the smugness of coupledom

A reluctant invitation to attend at their table
Generously delighting
In someone else's happiness
Then left brusquely on your own
To take a taxi home
At the end of the occasion
Resuming your life
As a single oddity

Will you not reach out to touch my hand
It's the hand of a baby
So that I can grasp at even your littlest finger
Inviting you to fan the spark of love to flame
I need to take delight
In the flicker of your smile
To be happily confirmed
In the mirror of your eyes
Can't you see that I have just begun
On the road that you have travelled
That today I need to hold onto you as guide
Will you be that other for me now
Until I find my feet
And grow tall as a sunflower
Under love's beaming smile

I need to believe in life
I need to believe in love
To experience even once in my lifetime an us

Do you remember when there was an us
Do you remember what the softest kiss felt like
Brushed with loving lips up over your tingling skin
Or the sweet smell of someone's body lying asleep beside you
Or the supportive touch of their hand as they held onto your heart
And broke it open before your startled eyes
Like a luscious fig
And did the both of you taste of it then
When love was new
In spring

Recall it to your mind
And tell me what it means to you
What love has meant across your lifetime
Tell me
Was the pleasure worth it
Tell me
Would you do it all again
Despite the pain
Will you tell me the truth
As much as I can bear
Of love and intimacy
And trust and sex
Tell me of the person that you loved
And who loved you
Once upon a time
When it was ever summer

To those who have given up on love
Unlock your secrets from the deep
Set them free to walk upon this earth
Like the tallest guardian angels
Flaming with the light of love
So that they can pierce your flesh once again with passion's sword
I know these prisoners are constrained within your heart
I know you are the poorer for living a half-life

The best of you smothered
Underneath the ashes of your loving achievement
Remember it now
And share it aloud
With those who have given up on love
Wear the clothes of the love story of your life
And look resplendent
Shining proud for me

I appeal to those who have given up on love
Please don't give up on us
It is never too late to continue to love
So please
Don't give up on you
And please
Don't you give up on me

Auburn – For Mary

Faced with my helplessness
Not knowing how to help
I placed my hand under his elbow
And welcomed Ferdia home

We were married once
We have three children together
We found ourselves at a place
Where he didn't want to be

It hurts too much to be intimate
Now that this has happened again
I have some idea what it means
To have hope stolen
To fear for the future
So I touch him lightly on the elbow
Knowing there's no cure

We communicate through writing
As though he were still absent
He types a reply on his laptop
Attempting to correct the predictor
And I get called away

The tragedy of losing a voice
Enduring the pain
Surviving
Alone with no redemption
Too much for anyone to bear

So I place my hand under his elbow
Helping Ferdia home

Celibate Men in Dresses

Celibate men in dresses
Have captured God
Like an exotic wild animal
They try to keep him caged
Behind the tall narrow walls of their tradition
They scarcely give God room to breathe in the darkness

For centuries celibate men in dresses
Have excluded the feminine
Yet the Holy Spirit is feminine
And always partakes in the joy of the trinity
The assumption of a real woman into heaven
Makes the balance two male plus two female
Four is God's whole number

Celibate men in dresses
Exist without irony
In a world of feudal overlords
And absolute monarchs
They expect to command our attention
While we get on with our lives
Too kind to tell them the truth
Too busy to be bothered
Oblivious that celibate men in dresses
Have been refused their intrusion
Into heterosexual relationships
Diverting attention instead
Onto their latest out group
Today they mount an unrelenting inquisition
Against gay people

The commandant at Buchenwald
Where homosexuals were persecuted to death
Also had a private zoo for exotic animals
God was at home there among his prisoners

No kissing of the ring
There is no sleight of hand that can cover over the crime
Of upholding an institution of mitred prelates
At the expense of innocent children abused
Celibate men in dresses
Have continually crucified God
Not only in the stranger
They have forbidden the second coming of his resurrection
In the magisterium of his chosen people
A designation withdrawn from Jerusalem
And now definitively lost to those in Rome
Because God cannot be contained
Whatever his sexuality

Celibate men in dresses
Are neither real men
Nor inferior substitutes for real women
Real men and women feel the breath of God's own spirit
On their naked skin as they make love
They set God free to play like the wind
And incarnate in their humanity
They grow up to be ordinary mothers and fathers
They are not infallible
They are never made into saints
But God entrusts his children to them
He shines out in the light of their eyes
He runs free in their fun and in their laughter
For love is where holiness is found

Young mothers and fathers are heroes of love
They sacrifice all for their little ones
Older men and women have proven their holiness
They give joyful service to others for the long haul
God is moving silently in the open hearts of his chosen people
He can be glimpsed in the warmth of their loving relationships

Weighed down like a millstone
With embroidered brocade and the finest lace
Celibate men wear dresses
Of the sheerest irrelevance
Because God has escaped their constraints
Untamed and unprotected
Always wild forever free
And celibate men in dresses
Guard cages that are empty
Nothing left to say
Because everything is frozen

In the end
There was no word

Gloria in Excelsis

Like a wise man following a star
I bring my gifts on Christmas Day
To the baby in the crib
I leave behind anxiety
Protect the cradled child from life's pessimism
If I no longer believe in a redeemer divine

Surrounded by the smell of pine and evergreens
I light a silent candle for the dead
Remembering the candle in the window
And the long ago welcome home on Christmas Eve

The children's story of no room at the inn
And the superstition of my grown-up sensibilities
Equally excluded from the humble scene within
I bring imaginative possibilities to the framing from without
Of a young mother and her newborn baby
A practical commitment to the business of the present
A careful reverence for life continuing on
Discerning mystery amidst the ordinary straw

This Christmas Day has been born in Bethlehem
A saviour
I am my own redeemer

I whisper a prayer and muster help with hope
I say to the midwinter gloom of an empty universe
I am alive thank God
For those with whom I live and love
I can try to make things better
And bring glory to the highest heavens
Gloria in excelsis

Benedicite — For Jeanne and Mark

"Yes" is a courageous commitment
As delicate as the air that it displaces
To be received with reverence
And venerated for its holiness

"Yes" is an assent to life
An annunciation heard
Nine months before the nativity
A foundation stone upon which
To build a home within
"Yes" is a sacred word

She shyly proffered us the ring
A glittering diamond crystal
That seemed to be floating on air
"We got engaged this Christmas Eve" she said

They both were beaming happily
Inviting praise and recognition
Commending themselves to each other
And to us for their achievement

"I had a dream that I was choosing children's names" he said
"Middle-class names of saints like Paul and Mark
She was sure of the ring in the window
So I asked her to marry me"
And she said "Not like this not now outside a jeweller's shop"
And then she said "Why not"

Such is the logic of how lives intertwine
The pattern of how decisions are arrived at

Commitments that are timed to coincide irregularly
Cut like the facets of a diamond ring
Facing away from each other
For a whole lifetime of continuous hope

"Yes" a feather-light kiss to the forehead
"Yes" a whispered grace
"Yes" the tenderest of looks
And a determined proclamation
"Yes" is the bravest undertaking
Of all the continuous covenants

For unto is born from heaven above
On every Christmas morning our lives
Love the divine redeemer
Benedicite
Say "Yes"

Epithalamion: A Poem for Terry

When I grow old and have no voice
No children there to care or to remember me
I shall always know
That there was once a midsummer's day in Dublin
When I was loved

Then I shall smile in the dreamtime
Hearing once more
The dawn chorus announced with trumpet blasts
And see the vivid roses burst into bloom
And twine around the morning of that glorious day in June
When I was finally allowed
To be loved

I shall laugh inside through Stephen's Green
And leave my dancing footsteps in the dew
So you can follow me
And take your place
By my side
On a day which was prepared
Since the beginning of the world
For you are my world
And I have always loved you

Whenever I would look into your questioning eyes of blue
To find myself reflected in your goodness
I could never feel afraid of others' judgement
Or their shame at these extolling words
As true as you have proved to be
For an everyday eternity
Of table fellowship and fun

The sun swept to attention and saluted us at noon
We did not stand in one another's shadow
When we vowed either to each
Three times before our family of like-minded friends
Who have supported us for better or for worse

The words were tolling in the golden air
They bathed us in light so that we shone
I shall honour you with my esteem
Because of your integrity
I promise to support and bear the weight
Of your open unprotected soul
I promised too to love you
As if ever I had stopped
And needed to commence what is continuous
And round as the ring you gave to me
Blessed with your affection

On that laughing summer's day
The wind was cheering
And the leaves on the trees were waving
As we processed towards our future through O'Connell Street
Side by side we laid our bouquet of roses
Out at the GPO
Acknowledged those who gave their lives
So we could be cherished equally
Proclaimed ourselves free
And free to become better together
Than either of us could choose to achieve on our own
And we withdrew relevance
From those who disapproved
Of our new and mutual
Republic of love

There is nothing I regret more than my compliance
That I was not in my life more undignified
And reckless and awkward
Like you a fearless fighter
Joyfully at home in foreign lands
An encourager of dreams
An explorer of the soul's secrets
And warm and tender as the pleasure of our private trysts

Whenever we shall be no more and nobody remembers us
These words of mine shall inherit the earth
They will echo in the heart of every season
That there was once a midsummer's day in Dublin
When I was loved
And they will sing out loud my song
Repeat publicly the poem I have told about you
And the treasure you endowed me with
The inestimable adventure of a meaningful life

This simple shining truth shall belong to you immortally
That once upon a time
On a Dublin midsummer's day at noon
I always loved you

Then you will be moving in the wind and in the trees
And especially when the roses are in bloom
You will gladden with a smile or with a glance
When people feel your presence in the wonder of beautiful words
Lingering in a room like your fragrance
The blown petals falling to earth like prayers
Whispering over and over that I have always loved you
That I
Have loved you
Too

We cast a vote for love
We changed the landscape
We made a space on this tiny isle of saints and scholars
For the world

A Vote for Love

A Note from the Artist

THIS POEM REFERS TO THE Marriage Referendum in Ireland: "The people of Ireland have voted yes for everyone …" So I created a see-saw. The terrain and lie of the land was not even since it was an uphill battle for gay people in Ireland. Homosexuality was only decriminalized in 1993, the year I graduated in architecture from UCD. So the bottom of the composition shows an un-level landscape. But the see-saw is level. In equilibrium. Equal. Fair. On the left are lots of hearts. The good and decent hearts of the Irish people who voted yes. Without them that see-saw would not have risen to equilibrium. I made a linocut stamp to create the heart especially and used pigment ink. On the right a verdant representation of green and lush landscape, and two gold rings, the symbol of marriage. The work is graphically inspired and narrative driven and straddles between abstraction and figuration.

COLIN EATON.

Gentle reader,

This second collection is entitled *A Chaplet of Roses*. The name comes from a poem I wrote about my mother's death. The death of parents is an experience which faces all of us:
> "Thankfulness for setting me free
> To appreciate our differences
> My ambivalence
> I'm aware you managed that well …"

The collection contains *A Vote for Love*, a poem about the marriage equality referendum:
> "We cast a vote for love
> We changed the landscape
> We made a space on this tiny isle of saints and scholars
> For the world"

My Perfect Ruby was written for my friends Vickie and Conor to celebrate the birth of their baby. The concluding verse expresses universal parental desires for the future:
> "My wish is as a young Ruby woman
> Blazing with light and rich with the Cork colours
> You'll never have to comply nor compromise yourself
> Or worse withdraw from all that life's adventure has to offer
> My hope is when you fly the nest
> You'll inhabit your heritage
> And soar with widespread wings of unconcern
> To become a true rebel always …"

May the poems in this book serve as an inspiration to recapture the confident exuberance of youth!

With every good wish,

MICHAEL MURPHY

Flora and Fauna

And When You Speak of Trees

I plant a tiny tree in crumbling earth
And make an investment
In someone else's future

When I leave this world
I know my representative will be a mighty oak
With wide-spreading penetrating roots
And branches that can soar into the sky's embrace
A worthwhile legacy to have left behind me

It signifies that I believe in a life hereafter
That I believe in you whom I've never met
A leap of faith that you shall care for trees
And the animals and birds who live within its leafy shelter

In an unimaginable future
You too shall be my representative on earth
You shall speak up for trees
Even though you never knew
That I was the one who dug the hole
Loosened the roots and gently settled the ball down into clay
And staked the sapling's stem
When it was my time under the sun

You shall be my voice as well
To husband what I had intended

Your time is now when living is all
And love I hope that you found love
In your relationship with trees
As I did once in mine

It turns out that love is the firmest groundwork of our being
With roots to anchor truth
That love grows up to be a mighty oak tree
Linking the earth to the heavens
And those who have gone before to the present generation
With no beginning and no projected end
An oak tree is eternity for an everyday

And when you speak of trees and give them breath
A breeze will move imperceptibly through clacking branches
Listen then to the chattering whisper of their leaves
You'll find that trees have the ability to soothe the soul
With their conversation
With their assured presence
With their sudden silences
With their waiting
For humble trees are wise
They tap deep into the earth
They remind us when we're inundated by life's political trivia
Of the one enduring strength that truly matters
The unconditional love that surrounds us
Love that can be seen and heard in oak trees
In those who planted them
And in those others who will tend
To help them grow to independence

Anna's Dog Toga

I believe a dog should be a he
A suitable companion for a man
Terry corrects me "Toga is a she!"
So I told him I prefer to think of her
As trans-gendered like Bruce Jenner

Mind you from behind
She walks like a model
Toe first heel next
Waggling her booty like jello
From side to side

Though from the front
Her hind legs are as powerful
As a rugby player's in a ruck
Try taking her out for a sedate stroll
On the scent for overlooked pieces of bread

And what do you make of her behaviour
Coming in at two o'clock in the morning
Some tramp from God knows where
"Honey, I forgot the time ..." Slut
Charging down the hall
And launching herself from the top step
Onto Terry in the bed licking him all over
Slurp slurp slurp like her last drink in some cheap speakeasy
You think a kiss will make this better?
As beautiful as Marilyn in the striptease spotlight
Who could refuse her anything?
Nevertheless I keep getting the fuzzy end of the lollipop
I think I'll sue for loss of consortium

She has to be gay
Or at the very least bisexual
Maybe she's a lesbian
A he or a she or a tranny
As Osgood said "Well, nobody's perfect!"

A chocolate Labrador named Toga
Whose soulful looks melt all before her
Whose motivation is food and hunting cats
And two paw hugs retrieving hearts
Loved and shared by Anna and by Terry
And luckily by me for being the shadow's chosen one
Two females who are loved by two males
A perfect foursome family

Bad Behaviour Can Get Elephants Killed

Animals do not belong to us
They allow us to live near them
And bad behaviour can get elephants killed

I saw Tyke an African elephant
Running free in 1994
Through the business streets of Honolulu
Not on the tropical savannahs of home
Before Hawaiian police shot her dead
With eighty-seven bullets
In front of horrified bystanders
One went in through the eye
Never to be forgotten

The elephant and us
We saw too much
Of man's inhumanity
To fellow creatures

The female died in a hail of gunfire
Because she would not accept
Being imprisoned in a circus
Wearing ridiculous costumes
Turning tricks for man's amusement

For twenty years she suffered the insistent cruelty of clowns
Then she lashed out and killed a trainer
She had to be put down
No question

The public must be protected
From a female on the rampage
Especially an elephant
Because of her intelligence
And her memory
And the bigness of her heart

Animals do not belong to us
They allow us to live near them
To be graced by their honour
To learn from their integrity
To encourage gentleness
And lay hold of tenderness
To allow ourselves to love them
And be loved a hundredfold in return
Only then can we appreciate and fight for freedom
For everyone

Animals do not belong to us
They allow us to live near them
And bad behaviour can get elephants killed

Poems for Friends

Seven

When I was seven
I deliberately kicked the ball into the road
When I was seven

And my friend ran after it
When I was seven

Too late I saw the roaring truck
My friend frozen in the road
I heard the thump the screaming brakes
The pumping blood red
When I was seven

And I saw that it was all my fault
When I was seven

They could not put him together again – no
My best friend – no
When I was seven

They said that he was now an angel
Because I kicked the ball out into the road
When I was seven

He was me and I was he
My best friend who ran away
And went to heaven without me
When I was seven

And I thought that I could never speak again
Ever again

never again
I lost my voice
When I was seven

Later on when bullies mocked me
Co-copied my st-stammer
I stood there frozen unable to say
Anything back quick-fire
Some devastating put-down
That began without a vowel
Or a consonant just a hard scream
So I thumped my attackers
But each time I died a little more
Inside

And then when I was forty-seven
I recognised my best friend
When I was forty-seven

She was kind and good with children
She took all the time to hear me
And I began to speak again
When I was forty-seven

I knew that I would never have to stammer in her presence
Ever again
Forever
When I was forty-seven

I am able to say
My voice came back
When I was forty-seven

So I said yes to you
Yes I do

94

Yes I will
It took only a breath yes
And it was easy
For love never dies between a boy and his best friend

This Easter the two of us are risen from the dead
A man has regained his voice through an angel from heaven
Dressed in white and holding a bouquet of seven red roses

We have promised to protect each other with love
On our journey towards the future
For seven times seven years
Or for as long as the time will allow

So side by side talking together
Me and my best friend
We walk deliberately now
Out into the open road

My Perfect Ruby

When I looked you in the eye
My perfect Ruby
I knew that you were here
To cure diseases
To change base metal into bars of gold
And to prolong my life indefinitely
A panacea
She lamped at me and said
"See ya
On Pana!"

More precious than diamonds
I cupped your head in my hand
As you thrust into the cradle of my love
Glowing red hot with life
Supping at my breast
And I named you Ruby Ryan
After your dad
Who did the same

C'mere my perfect Ruby –
You took us by surprise girl
When you landed here la –
Da berries – a welcome gift like – on-real

Look at the gatch of you
Lying on your back with your doonchie arms in the air
A bold Cork ball-hopper all balmed out

And from the tocht in my throat
I knew my perfect Ruby

I just knew that as a family
When your ship arrived into the safe harbour of our Lee-side shore
That we were all haunted like

As I swaddle you with wealthy words from Cork
My desire for you girl
Is to create a limitless world of possibilities
In which you can play happily for an eternity
To construct a safe reality ring o' rosie round you
Chainied up with loving language
From your mam and from your dad
That you can trust implicitly

Where as much as we can make it happen
You will be free to be yourself forever
To love and break boys' hearts on Barracka
And to be loved unconditionally in return

My wish is as a young Ruby woman
Blazing with light and rich with the Cork colours
You'll never have to comply nor compromise yourself
Or worse withdraw from all that life's adventure has to offer
My hope is when you fly the nest
You'll inhabit your heritage
And soar with widespread wings of unconcern
To become a true rebel always
My perfect Ruby
O precious daughter of mine

She lamped at me again and laughed
"C'mon boy willa chalk it down!
Amn't I the bulb off you both?
And amn't I ever –
Up the rebels! –
A proud daughter
Of Cork"

On Food

Bread

For Jayne in Spain

Bread should be a shared pleasure
Preferably with a loved one
Breaking a loaf open
You have to taste some of this
Delicious
Smell it
What do you think?

Thank you for being here with me
For making the loneliness go away for a moment
For letting me laugh and cry
Try that black one there
Is it rye with molasses maybe?
Have you had it with salt and olive oil?
Isn't bread such a shared pleasure

I can hardly ask these questions of myself
At home on my own
I never buy bread to eat all alone
Staring at the wall in my kitchen
Listening for the cat
Waiting for the mobile phone to ring
I do sometimes wait I mean
For an invitation to go visit
Bread is such a shared pleasure
The sheer goodness of it
Don't waste it
Eat up while you can
There are people starving
Did I thank you for inviting me?

Oh they've brought us a new basket
Hot crusty bread wrapped up in a napkin
You really must have some of this
Go on even a little piece
I love to see the crumbs
The way it breaks apart
I'd eat bread every day if I was able
At someone else's table if I could
Wouldn't that be heavenly
Sat here with a friend
Who cares like you
Bread is such a shared pleasure

Figs and Blue Cheese

Figs and blue cheese
Waiting on Wedgwood plates
Under a white sun umbrella
A table set by the pool
Swimming in summer heat

Salty cheese and succulent figs
Overflow a cracked Cartuja plate
Under an ancient olive tree
Shading a rough board from the scalding sun
Capturing each delicate breeze as ever

Ripe green figs and strong blue cheese
Tasting sweet and crunchy creamy
An eternal offering from the gods
A gift today for you and me
To share with love and be inspired by

The Kiwi

I think the kiwi
Such an unnecessary fruit
Like an unripe green tomato
The last piece of a salad
To be left behind in a bowl
An unlovely rejected afterthought
To be scraped into the bin

I grew up without the kiwi
So why should I include it now
In my food
In my environment

Kiwis arrived in England in the fifties
But I never remember them in Castlebar
A sliced addition to a tired leaf of lettuce
Winking repulsively like a gleaming eye
Desiring to be eaten alive

The kiwi is such an unnecessary fruit
About as useful as a decorative kumquat

On Death and Dying

I Shall Die

There will come a time
When I shall die
And be obliterated

On that momentous day
Which will matter to no one else but me
The meaning I gave to the furniture of my life
Will fade with my ghost

The pictures I collected the china I chose
The book I was reading my toothbrush
Stuff to be binned with the dead body in the bed

I was an unimportant person
The generation who met me
Freed from duty
Will soon forget

Nevertheless I was loved once
By someone special
And I loved him in return
We glimpsed eternity together
Before all traces of existence
Were wiped away by oblivion

Enough

These are the final days
Trembling on the brink
Before my life
And what we have done together
The love story we have made
Overflows into eternity

I feel sadness
At having to leave that love behind
Love was all that mattered
In the end

And I regret my abandonment
Of you and me
Facing into this final act
That I shall do unusually alone

Death will happen to me unbeknownst
For once without my love
Fiercely protecting me to that uttermost breath
Beyond exhaustion
And the sudden unexpected silence
Of that sundering moment of change
When I shall flow through your loosening fingers
Like water
An exhalation towards the ultimate
Setting me and our love story free forever
To soar over an ocean of grief

I shall surprise you at times
And overwhelm you at others

But it's me just saying "Hi there!"
As our loving memories re-play on a loop
Without ever ceasing

I shall breathe you in my love
With my last living breath
And take the strength of your glorious spirit with me
Into eternity

But I shall need to say when I'm gone
What you cannot bear to hear
That the two of us
You and me
That we have done
Enough

Interruption

I think I should sit down for Death
Such an ill-mannered interruption
Deserves to be received seated

To place a full stop in mid-sentence
Is offensive and meaningless
It leaves me nonplussed

Patching tentative presence onto such an absence
Voicing into the void
Attempting to cover over the hole in existence
With a tissue of words and phrases
Sounds courageous
Even foolhardy
But bound to rend
Inevitably
Finally

Nevertheless I shall sit down for Death
As a personal protest
To uphold a standard of behaviour
Since I do know better

Good manners should matter
At least to me

Hail and Farewell

There is grief buried deep within
Misplaced pain heavy and burdensome

When I read out loud emotional poems
Sorrow surfaces suddenly in the absent space
Between the words
Ave atque vale

I have difficulty holding on
Holding back
Riven
Hiccupping inappropriate sobs
A fury of stinging tears
Heartbroken
I never knew I was

When I listen to music
Bach beautifully rendered
Returned restored handed over
I cry at so munificent a gift
When I hear a brass band
I laugh and weep together
At the trumpeting valour
Head held high pennants flying
Terry doesn't mind anymore
I don't know why that happens

When I packed the car in Spain
For the journey home
Toga the Labrador my shadow
Was absent

I found her sunk in the well of the car
At the passenger seat where I usually sat
Woebegone
She knew what parting meant
She sensed my heart breaking
Broken
Take me with you
I embraced her
And she licked my beard

When my mother died
She was ninety-five
Sleeping and not eating
A tiny figure curled among the pillows
With her head resting into her shoulder
Like a famished fledgling *scalltán*
I kissed her goodbye
And left
I never saw her alive again
I can never give that knowledge
Voice

Relationships Do Not Die

Relationships do not die with death
They live on in our bones
They are a part of who we are each day
Participating in the conversation
Living still
Whispering

Their shades visit while we are asleep
In search of home
Renewing feelings from the past
Enabling us to face the future
In the present
Helping with their gifts

I can forgive and accept them for who they were
I do not feel diminished by who they thought I was
They are alive
Always benevolent
They die only when I die

Relationships do not die with death
They live on in our bones

Some Personal Poems

The Seeker

I am a seeker after truth
Shooting arrows at a moving target
Capturing truth with an onslaught of words
Whose whittled tips sink home
With the exploding poison of emotional recognition

Refining my aim over time
I have improved in my endeavour
To build a layering of phrases
To create a language barrier
Both protective and offensive
A problematic personal reality
Open to challenge and dispute
Because you do not see me
From the place where I see you

Situate in that resistant gulf
Exposed to instant judgement
No regard for wisdom earned
Irrelevant as a used hankie
I can lose my certain footing
And fall forever in infinite space
Without another's holding lifeline

Truth requires the two of us
Communicating in a hail
Of shooting arrows building up
Or taking down word by word
I need you to help me
Tell the truth
Lacking your support

I lie
I speak false

Overcome my reticence
Shoot arrows at my heart
Seek me out my love
As I have sought out you
And let us be true to one another
Striking arrows at the target
Together

On Turning Sixty-five

Nothing to prove
Nothing to lose
An everything to do list:

Insist on being here
Write
Creatively play every day
Stay offline
Embrace an electronic sunset

Don't follow time
Potter
Have a project
Life-long learning top of the agenda
Art and literature
Listening to classical music

Revolt and don't comply
Become an annoying individual
Drop people who aren't supportive
Love the few
Be truthfully rude to interfering relatives
And take the time to contemplate
Life and death without regret or bitterness
Enjoy the holiday here
Always
Or at least
For as long as possible
And live today eternally

Bereft

I feel bereft of God
No resting place left for my idealism
No deity to invoke
No divine being to call upon for help

When Helen and her sister attended a Catholic Mass
The standing and the sitting the incense and solemnity
They got the giggles: "Presbyterians sit and pray!" they complained
I'd never seen the spectacle as ridiculous before
Which it is – and a waste of time – if you don't believe

At least I have the language still
To express impossible truths and capture the ineffable
To underpin my life with meaningful myths
The birth of immanence
The crucifixion of truth
The resurrection of hope
And perhaps that final stage of growing up
The ascension to mature human responsibility
Without the joyful presence of my God
With all the sharp-eyed clarity of a Presbyterian elder

Belfast

Yesterday I went up to Belfast
There were churches on practically every street
With unfamiliar names like Moravian and Plymouth Brethren

In Sainsbury's supermarket in Sprucefield
They had short-crust pastry pies
Foods that we would never even think of eating

A lot of the white people's facial types were very different
Alien to my eyes foreign

Belfast must be populated with the relics of empire
What Dublin was like once
In the time of James Joyce
Before we became an independent people's republic
And the eventual exodus of English gentry
Leaving us the poorer for their absence
And presence

Complicity

Were I to remain silent
Where there is injustice
I would be complicit in a crime

How can you consider that black and white are equal
But treat them as separate nonetheless
How can you regard women the same as men
But still insist that they have different roles to play
How do you condemn people who are gay
But hold them in respect and with dignity

When I hear such distinctions
Bullying subtly with buts
Do I not recognise
The suffering of one like me
Do I not reach out
To shield from shame
My brother my sister myself
And dare I name their rationalisation
An opinion that was formed in advance
Prejudice

Email to ISIS

Hi ISIS

I see you have a passion for ignorance
Which is why you behead people
To cleanse the world of knowledge

Because you consider culture a decadent concept
You blow up works of art
To obliterate antiquities and the past

Since for you women are less than men
You blank them with burqas
Negating their existence
Confining them behind closed doors

If women bring children to school
They must have a male chaperone
Otherwise you throw them off the highest building
In the name of Allah the most merciful
A god who according to you demands human sacrifice
And the rape and murder of apostates and infidels

You know ISIS it's the usual story of religion
From the history you excised
The Crusaders the Catholic Monarchs,
Cromwell the Inquisition
The intolerant have always engaged in wars of religion
I wish we had grown up a little more
And abandoned those primitive opinions
For that is what they are: paradoxical ideas
That are true and not true at the same time
Undecidable metaphors that some people choose to live by

Which helps them to be healthy human beings

I regret to say you're nothing special
People like you have always existed
Hitler and Stalin Pol Pot and Mao Tse Tung
Kim Jong Il and Isaias Afwerki in Eritrea
Tyrants who take their peoples hostage
And experiment with terror and mass murder

When you have finished
Re-making the world in your image yet again
Turning this verdant earth into a barren desert
May I ask will there be room in your creation
For those who sing and dance
And sculpt and paint and make music
Write with beautiful words and tell emotional stories
Who value the human spirit
The freedom of the imagination
Who take delight in the plurality of peoples
Who place their trust in love and live their dream
Or will those few left alive who vehemently disagree with you
Be refugees fleeing the handiwork of a barbarian

I feel sorry for your parents
Who found a welcome refuge in Europe
You have rejected the opportunities they gave you
Returning to the poverty they fled
How can they be proud of what you have now become
A dangerous deluded madman
Psychotically certain of your righteousness
In need of serious intervention

I can see why you wield such control
You are terrified of what's inside you
Of what's inside each one of us

You torture others with the blackness in your own soul
Externalise the evil at your core
In a desperate attempt to save yourself
Blaming God for giving in to badness
Needless to say I don't believe in your justification

How could you be sane
With your suppression of women
Your refusal of the feminine side of your nature

The greatest contribution I can make to humanity
Is to manage myself in a positive way
Allowing others do the same in their way
At their own pace accepting difference
I dare not let your madness contaminate me
I need strong boundaries to protect myself
For lunacy is alive like quicksand
If I walk in there I'll drown

Health is a personal journey undertaken within
An ethical achievement to be worked for day by day
Hardly made easy by going overseas to Syria
It's not a simple task but a worthwhile endeavour
The benefits are felt daily in my dealings with people

So I appeal to the best in you
Even though I know you cannot hear me
Imprisoned as you are in your passion for ignorance
I hope that you will find peace
Eventually

Michael

Repetition

When there's no alternative
I'll try again

I have made wrong decisions in my life
And I am scalded with regrets
About the past

About what has not happened in the future
Continuing on till infirmity or death
I feel fear

Yet everything that has happened
Is the same: it just happened on different days

Free floating anxiety
Not tied down to something specific
Ties me up in knots
A linguistic net of language
That catches insignificant gnats
Over and over again

I survived and got myself to here
By finding solutions to actual problems
Practically as they happened to me

Why do I forget that truth
Continually

Devotion

I am devoted to you
This motivation gives meaning to my life
It has illumined everything I do

So thank you for choosing me
To love
To be intimate with
To carry like a cloak
The reflection of your open soul

Where there is love
Despair does not venture in
Where there is affection
Forgiveness happens unbeknownst
Where there is laughter
We are equal and as one

When I caress your face with my finger
Trace the delicate hairs of your eyelids
Touch your lips with the gentlest kiss
Embrace your strong body
When I hold you to me in my arms
I carry what is most valuable in all the world
Access to your presence

I benefit from that burden
It clears a pathway for me through life's dangers
To your heart

I shine in the light of your acute mind
I see myself reflected in your gaze

I hear myself at home in your kindly speech

Inspired by those blessings
I can occupy my chosen place
Caring for your well-being

To become a unique individual
Different from you
Connected loosely
Yet solidly belonging

The two of us transfigured
By the deepening of intimacy
And the abundant flowering of our love

The Mayo Sequence

Home to Mayo

I am a Mayo man born and bred
I have the character of a Mayo native
Who hails from the plain of the yew trees

My ancient roots are silently asleep
Beneath the brown blanket bog of Ballycroy
Untold ages of my Mayo ancestors
Are compressed within my tight-grained rings
Their umbilical-corded branches linking clay with sky
Have combined in a stout *meitheal*
To grow a dark indomitable tree that is eternally evergreen
Whose flattened leaves reach heavenwards in the racing Mayo light
Protecting those who went before
On their climbing pilgrimage home

I am a dowsing rod of yew
I am the resurrection welling up
From successive imprints on my soul
They have written their names on my body
Like the ancient ogham inscriptions on the standing stones
Of Erris and Murrisk and Costello
A shin bone with five fingers across it meaning "I: the yew tree"
We have survived through countless lifetimes
In the nine baronies of Mayo

Green sapwood for the tension
Red heartwood for compression
Wood that is gnarled and tough
And as mightily resilient as the people of Mayo have had to be
These are my people
This is my place

We have renewed like the yew tree over thousands of years

Mayo handseled me the flame of life
I stand indebted for that gift of highest value
The flesh of your flesh in an eternal relay
Mayo people I know instinctively from deep within
Today it is my turn to give them voice
To make known in my living all of their untold stories
For the West is awake in me
I am a Mayo man born and bred
I have the character of a Mayo native
Who hails from the plain of the yew trees

Though I left the county years ago for work around the world
I could never settle or commit to life elsewhere
Inside I always feel an outsider misplaced
In my mind I always live at home in Mayo

Welcomed home now for the Christmas
By a candle in the window decked with green holly red berries
Or maybe wondering in London or Boston
In Toronto or Melbourne
Is there snow on Neiphin or abroad on the top of Mweelrea

Building summer sandcastles now at Keel in Achill with the next generation
Walking the golden beach at Old Head with the previous one
Or maybe crowding into foreign bars
Proudly flying the red and green amongst expatriate Irish
Almost afraid to watch Mayo in the final
Trying their utmost giving of their best yet again
Unwilling to submit to a surrender

Mostly I miss the warm embrace of the Mayo accent
That kiss on the lips blowing in off the Atlantic with the sea spray

Soft and fierce and salty easy
Mayo talk is a baptism that strengthens my spirit
It fills me with hope and immerses me in certainty
It welcomes me into the family of like-minded people
I feel wrapped up in the arms of Croagh Patrick surrounding Clew Bay
With the church at the summit worn aslant
Carried at a typical angle of western defiance

I'm aware that spoken words in Mayo
Mean more than what they say
There are many layered voices speaking
If you traverse the talk on the *tóchar Phádraic*
Avoid the *fóidín mearaí*
Attend to the codes once hewn from a tree trunk of yew
And be careful of the truth for fear of the oppressor
I know the Mayo way
I have climbed the Reek *Dia is Muire linn*

I remember especially those faithful Mayo patriots
Who fought for their freedom at the Races of Castlebar
First citizen President John Moore's republic
Founded on being free to tell the whole truth without fear
And with liberty fraternity equality for all
Their voices were suppressed and silenced by the enemy
Their unwavering Mayo spirit is alive and can never be defeated
Their souls are resurrected when Mayo wins
Their souls are resurrected when Mayo loses
They are alive in us when we give of the best in ourselves
They live forever like the yew tree when we attend to the truth
When we value it voice it tell it and flaunt it like the red and green
For their memory's sake we can never permit a default or defeat
Today in the Mayo capital of Castlebar
We owe them the freedom to speak in the fullness of truth
To let each Mayoman have his say without fear in this republic

I am a Mayo man born and bred
I have the character of a Mayo native
Who hails from the plain of the yew trees
Today I have renewed my yew tree roots
Today I have reclaimed my Mayo heritage
These are my people
This is my place
Today I have come home
To Mayo

A Vote for Love

The people of Ireland have voted for me
A homosexual man
They recognised my place
They set me in a broad street

Irish people brought the new law into being
That I have an equal right
To marry the person of my choice
They redeemed the word love in humanity's constitution

The Mammies and the Daddies
The Grandpas and the Nanas
Wrote yes: my child is cherished
The same as any other

My mother wrote yes to love
She affirmed her love for her son
That it was unconditional
She nourished me by writing yes for my lifetime

My father wrote yes to me
He underpinned my being with a covenant
A solemn agreement handed on
From father to son

I grew up gay in Castlebar
Beyond the limits of language
Displaced in a world without words
A disgraced outsider
Shamed by my nameless desires

French literature delivered me salvation
Book learning that privileged absence
Reader and writer both invoking death
Yet looking to speech as a present possibility

Saint Genet and Gide and Albert Camus
Stole creative fire from the gods
To illuminate my inner Mayo
With Mediterranean descriptions
Of illegal sexual encounters underground

Of beautiful male bodies
Swimming provocatively in summer heat
Of exotic Parisian queens
Trailing miracles of the baroque like furbelows
Of imagining a solitary Sisyphus absurdly happy
Climbing to the top of a cold Croagh Patrick

Pioneering writers wrote upon my soul
They inscribed the vellum of my skin with sexual traces
They founded me in a reality that fit
They endowed me with a language of affirmation
They grounded me in fraternity
As one who is equal to another

These words I wear have set me free
They worked on mothers and fathers
Constituency by constituency

On those young people home to vote
Gathered on board their boat
Sailing into Dublin singing
"She moved through the fair …"

They flew from Ghana and Los Angeles

To cast a ballot for their faggot family
From Hong Kong and San Francisco
To demand freedom for their queer friends
I watched the televised map turn green
As the chakra of the heart began to flow

The floodgates of Dublin Castle opened after the vote
And a rainbow of language inundated Dame Street
Men holding hands with men
Women holding hands with women
Men and women holding hands
Lovers out in public walking above ground

They came from north and south and east and west
Linking chains of cheering men and women
Celebrating absence presence difference sameness
Dancing waving kissing embracing crying
A cacophony of car horns and sirens blaring
The unstoppable tide of a proud nation
Urging forward into welcoming acceptance
Joy radiating outwards into the relief of speech
At last a manumission and release of fellow prisoners
At long last recognition and performance
For the limitless language of love
Only silent churchmen barricaded dusty doors
Against the greening breath of the Holy Spirit
And the swelling surge of sexual truth

It was a Katherine and Ann Louise day
Who asked to have their Canadian marriage
Recognised by Irish courts a decade ago
A love they both proclaimed and named
A life they proudly lived out loud
They asked just to be included
Not to be erased by a knowing consensus

On that joyous Saturday all the people approved
The two women threw their open hearts to the audience
And we caught them gratefully
Overturning years of hurtful judgements
In the stroke of a pen

The people of Ireland have voted yes for everyone
They accepted into words what was not spoken
They acknowledged men and women who are Irish and gay

We cast a vote for love
We changed the landscape
We made a space on this tiny isle of saints and scholars
For the world

A Chaplet of Roses

Beneath the shadow of Croagh Patrick
In a lapping sea of lace
Head raised eyes closed
You gently floated away from shore
Towards the hope of the rising sun

A shaft of sunlight laid emphasis
On the structure of your sunken face
Presenting tight against the sufferings of old age

Your effigy infused an ordinary morning
With all the rainbow colours of a mother's love
In an extraordinary daily miracle

I understood that you were favoured
I knew you were ordained a saint

Weighed down with giving
I watched until you sank
The blast hit before the absent surface calmed
And then I turned and faced the land

Stripped of a welcome
No resting place left
With nobody to tell
The crowbar brigade has brought death to a sound foundation
A momentary fearful glimpse of what this clearance means

I have lost someone
Who loved me
Unconditionally

At Old Head where we'd look at the sea
I lit a beacon by the shoreline
A signal fire to show my love
For the young woman who became my mother

An eternal flame to prove my gratitude
For creating me in your image
For gifting me yourself
For as long as you drew breath

Thankfulness for setting me free
To appreciate our differences
My ambivalence
I'm aware you managed that well

Able to be proud declaring
You are my mother
I am your son
We have cared for each other
During two overlapping life-times
And now I am without

I pray that the alchemy of fire
May burn off the dross in our relationship
A purgatory of my own making
Since you never burdened me with expectations

The embers glow with the love you have nurtured
May the light guide your pilgrim's journey home

Refracted and reflected in the sea spray
You came to me across the foam
Wearing a white cloak and a coronet of golden roses
You didn't speak but held me in your gaze
As once you cradled your first-born in the curve of an arm

I stood in the rain reciting a decade of the rosary
With the beads you gave that my father owned

The tide on the turn shovelled up the sand
And you were gone from me
For ever

At my feet
A chaplet of roses
Floating gently on the ebb

Thank you
For your legacy
Of love

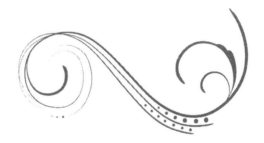

And we create our own universe
Redeemed by your eternal spirit
From the world of words that you have handled
So that we see butterflies in your beard too
Federico

LORCA WITH WHITMAN'S BUTTERFLIES

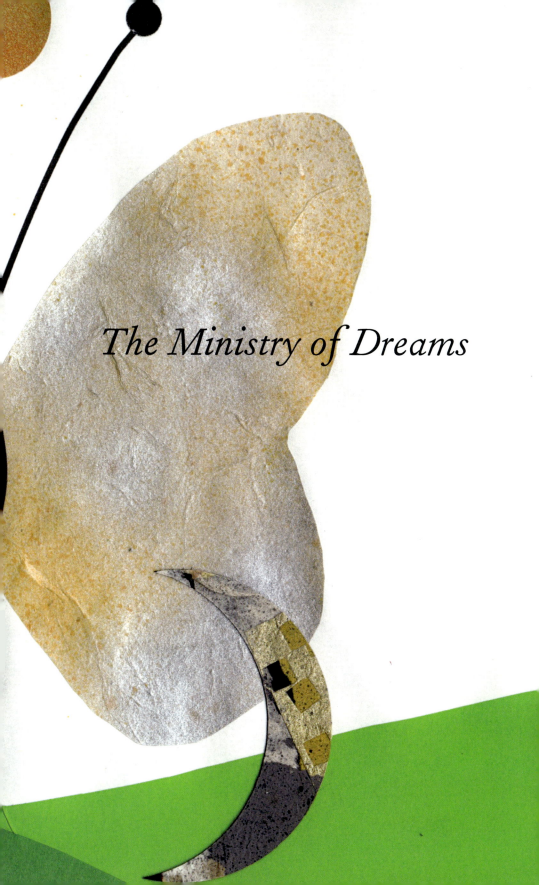

The Ministry of Dreams

A Note from the Artist

MY WORK FOCUSES ON PAPER-CUTS and collages using techniques which I have been honing and developing. Cutting precise cuts and juxtaposing with tearings and layers. I created a butterfly symmetrical in shape and outline. To the left it is colourful and to the right is a gossamer filigree colour, a shadow of itself or an indication of the colourful being it is in potentiality and shortly will become.

COLIN EATON.

Gentle reader,

New poems make up this third collection called *The Ministry of Dreams*, after an opening phrase used by the Minister for Children and Youth Affairs, Dr. Katherine Zappone:

> "I am the Minster of children who dream
> Running through pastures of the imagination
> Surrounded by music rejoicing and love …"

The poems in this collection are full of love for my partner, for friends, for relatives who died, and for my chocolate Labrador:

> "To understand how love runs to catch us up
> And now accompanies us lightly every day
> Is a miraculous vision my dog has lived out in my presence
> So that I too have become a wonderful creature
> Loving and loved in her service
> Truly human
> And I am truly blessed"

I would like to believe as you explore these poems, some could be meaningful to you, expressing truths that have the power to initiate change. That is the beauty of speaking words and phrases aloud:

> "The good I did which brings forgiveness
> Which absolves me
> And makes me new
> Is that I have loved
> And been loved
> By you"

My hope is that the words in these poems will be a blessing.

They're given with love,

MICHAEL MURPHY

Toga the Chocolate Labrador

My Dog and the Meaning of Life

Does my dog ponder the meaning of life
Sometimes she looks at me solemnly
Sat motionless on the floor with sadness in her eyes
I wonder does she feel it all so pointless
Living her solitary existence next to mine
As my loyal and deeply affectionate companion

I worry constantly that I've let her down
By not answering when she sits on alert at the end of the kitchen
Begging for a treat or for an interesting walk
Soliciting love and I have failed her helplessness again
Superior in her unending forgiveness and disappointment
Her ghostly silence follows me around the home
Settling at my feet weighing the options
Questions to be chewed over obsessively in her mind

She is secure of her place in my love
As regards food she is an indiscriminate beguiling opportunist
The wider questions of desire evoke a slumping heartfelt sigh
Like what is it all about really
And whether the waiting around is worth it
For those few circular moments of dancing excitement

Her honey brown eyes give the game away
And we collude in a reply by me tickling her under the ear
While she licks my wrist in solidarity
And then sorrowfully she sleeps across my feet
To prevent us from ever leaving each other
Occasionally glancing up with one understanding eye
Does it get much better than this

And I Am Truly Blessed

My dog is such a wonderful creature
I am blessed to have her love me
Be a consecrated priest through her mediating service
With the otherness of nature and of instinct
Connecting the two of us to what I had once forgotten

The feelings excited by a strange and sensual being
Who rubs her fur against my naked skin
Seeking hands-on comfort in human touch
Offer consolation and ease in each other's company

She earnestly licks my beard my hand my knee
To show affection and appeal to me
For tenderness at close of day
Before she sleeps flat out across my feet
Trusting me with the burden of her rapid breathing
Gifting me responsibility for keeping her alive
Preventing me from ever having to leave her side

A mix of surprise and curiosity at her playful behaviour
Gutteral growling and snapping at splashes from the swimming pool
Afraid I am drowning perhaps afraid to dive in
Then worrying a beach towel after fighting off the drying
Followed by a blissful roll in the grass scratching her back
Energetically chasing light reflections on the terracotta tiles
Endlessly jumping and turning forwards and back to catch ephemera
Or like a visionary staring transfixed at a refraction high on a wall
A meaningful apparition she alone can see glancing towards me for belief
Barking out the messages for mankind from this mystical experience
Sometimes induces awe at the miracle of existence

The overwhelming drive of her hunt for cats
Tracing a scent in the air on the ground oblivious of me behind
Left running on after the frenzied chase has already begun
Being hauled along by the lead controlled by a pumped up dog
Wild in her desire to catch and dispatch a fellow creature
Holding her back by the collar from potential danger
Enduring her yelps and squeals of frustrated agitation
As the cat breaks free then nonchalantly strolls to safety
Under her hapless gaze
And vanishes

Two quixotic travellers exploring the forests of southern Spain
Sifting through the undergrowth of pine and oak with a quivering lip
To find a crust gulped in a flash "Drop it!"
Tricked you slinking along beside me head down guilty
Knowing she did wrong but willing to suffer the consequences
Of those few moments of emotional disharmony
That will surely pass in forgiveness during the long march home

I have respect and reverence for her intelligence
Presenting herself by my side at mealtimes
Eyes focused on my face licking her lips to remind me to feed her
She performs a dance of delight for my benefit when I say food
Turning round and around then bumping my legs and hands
As I move towards the bag of kibble on the hall table
Another final pirouette upsetting the rug
A charge outside to wait by the bowl salivating
Pour it in OK then wolf it down
So grateful afterwards good girl

Poking me into wakefulness with her cold nose and pulling paw
In case I should overlook the shivering excitement of her early morning walk
Standing expectantly in the hall with ears cocked head to one side
Sensing a trip in the car scanning me

Am I coming along as well
Of course my pet sweet pea

My dog is a very sensitive creature
On occasion she gets depressed
Feels lonely when I go away
Sunk in gloom unmoving on the floor of my bedroom
Looking up under lowered brows at the suitcases
She cannot be comforted
How could I do this to her
Once she could not be found
As I packed for the journey to Dublin
She was down in the well of the car on the passenger side
Drowned in sorrow hoping I'd take her with me
The one I love
And hatefully leave behind for weeks at a time
Wondering does she remember the hurt

Mostly my dog lives life in hope
Cheerfully optimistic about the surprises
Held within the unfolding of the everyday
Enthusiastic about what I might offer her curiosity
Trying to give her a meaningful life
Does she pray to me her saviour for her daily bread
Crossing her hind legs before she goes to bed
And when she wakes and sees me
Does she instantly forgive those who trespass against her
Do I play God the Father to her dog daughter nature

My dog is a predator and a scavenger
Mirroring mankind without the ten commandments
She kills pigeons by the pool
She never has enough food
And swallows anything edible immediately
She is loyally true to who she is

She can never disappoint the Lord
As her owner I willingly take on responsibility for any bad behaviour
Sacrificing myself for her well-being

I thrive because she believes in me
Rising at six with a reason to face the day
Sleeping at night having achieved her happiness
Like an unpunishable child I love my dog
Unconditionally
And she loves me

To be blessed with such good fortune in one lifetime
To understand how love runs to catch us up
And now accompanies us lightly every day
Is a miraculous vision my dog has lived out in my presence
So that I too have become a wonderful creature
Loving and loved in her service
Truly human

And I am truly blessed

Love Poems

A Poem for Terry

Will you marry me at Michaelmas
On Saint Michael the Archangel's feast
Through the years we've spent together
You have been my guardian dear
You are my warrior commander
By my side to light and guide
With your shining sword of righteousness
You cleared the way you led me safe
To the home that you have hallowed
In the refuge of your heart

Will you marry me at Michaelmas
On the day that I was born
Celebrate with me my namesake
At the feast of all the Angels
And on my seventieth anniversary
Give to me your clear assent
To spend remaining years together
As you did once those thirty-three
With me your loving friend your staunch companion

I pledge the whole of my life as dowry
To devote to your good completely
For what was then
For what is now
And for whatever in the future
There may be

Will you marry me at Michaelmas
On the day the summer ends
As the autumn is beginning

At this time of late transition
On this quarter day of Michaelmas
At the start of one last chance
Will you be bold with me and cheerful
Play the hero one more time
Vault the barrier to the arena
Turn your back on getting older
And trail your cape behind you
Across the golden sands of time
Acknowledging all supporters
With a nonchalant wave of your hand

Beyond this special day of Michaelmas
For whatever span of years that I may live
I shall incarnate for you my patron
To whom God's love commits me here
I promise to protect you from all evil
Be a promoter of your good
Bring your light to bear on darkness
Be the champion of your truth
I shall advocate your freedom
To be different from me
I will love that spirit in you
Love your soul and love your dreams
And set you free to be yourself
To be the best that you can be

I feel blessed to have been chosen
So grateful to be graced by God above
At Michaelmas and beyond
Or for as long as the both of us
May live
And laugh
And love

Loss

If I should lose you
If I should lose our future together
Then I would be lost
Forever

How could I continue to live
Through the bitterness of a nuclear winter
The social countryside around laid waste
Completely on my own inside
What would be the point of such suffering
Left remembering for eternity
The warmth of your body beside me
In the cold loneliness of a double bed

Forced to endure the poverty of your absence
Where once I had in my possession
The wealth of all the world in your protective presence
Your smile has become for me
The dawn of carefree summer days
Your blue eyes unlocked the secrets of my soul
Your touch has brought a healing to my body

What matters most going forward is you and me
And love as an ideal for us both
When we said yes to each other
We meant it in a continuous present
That yes has reconfigured the past
And guaranteed a future built on hope
Then your support became the grace
Which has made me capable of being
And I can never afford to lose that

Lack that
Be limited by that catastrophe
Because I love you
So very much

Elysium

The day I pay an elderly ferryman
For passage across the rivers Styx and Acheron
Arriving at the underworld's liminal shore
Unready for the day of my reckoning
By what measure can I enter Elysium

I'm aware I shall be asked what good I did in my lifetime
I must swear truth
Or be delivered speechless into Lethe's oblivion
There can only be one immutable
Unchanging eternal reply
To the good that I did in my lifetime
I have loved
And been loved
By you

I should have been a saint
It was expected according to the dictates of my childhood
But I lived as best I could
With the compromises and ambivalence
The self-deceptions and excuses
Then I met you and you mirrored back
A truer sense of myself
Encouraging the best

The good I did which brings forgiveness
Which absolves me
And makes me new
Is that I have loved
And been loved
By you

How I Could Help You

My partner asked me casually
"D'you think you might never get published again?"
His question provoked terror
My heart lurched at the panorama of devastation
Which appeared in front of me
In nightmarish post-apocalyptic detail

This must be what death feels like
Unable to take another breath
Oblivion

Terry's blue eyes were smiling ruefully
"Well … ?" he interrogated

I could not burden him with the truth
My utter desolation would flash freeze his soul
No words
Ever

I examined Terry's kindly face and stroked his cheek
The touch felt warm
It realigned my thinking

Terry's welfare is the most important value in my life
His love is the reason I've been called
My care of him is paramount
Although at times it requires patience

"I have to keep writing," I concluded
"The act of writing is so courageous
Each word is a heartfelt journey into the unknown …"

"I was wondering today how I could help you?"

"You are now
Being here with me
Patiently over countless years
Dear heart!"

Politics

Madam President

We had hoped to say
Madam President
Be America for me

Instead we were lumbered
With a dangerous madman
A *liúdramán*
Who projects his insane disorder onto those outside
Denouncing what he sees
There in the mirror
Refusing the responsibility of truth
Defiling our treasury of words with his lies
Undermining the reality of our world

You warned us about the deplorables
With their passion for ignorance
Of those who decide to disregard
Not to know to misunderstand
Who choose to negate
What first they would have had to affirm
In order to build a life secure in unawareness
Living next door to the truth of their devastated selves
In a grotesque caricature of Christianity
God-fearing gun-toting Trumpians

Millions foreclosed the good that Hillary Clinton offered
Choosing instead to elect Donald Trump
Is this what Republican America has become
Or always was beneath the Hollywood veneer
Stained with the original sin of stolen land
Raising African slaves to farm it

Installing the walls of apartheid
Engaging in extraordinary rendition
Torturing elsewhere
Always at war in a futile attempt to obliterate
The banished shadow of the American dream

Not my president
Not who we are at heart
Most definitely it is who we are now
Outside and in
We have become complicit in our own misrecognition
So disliking the reality of the beautiful soul
To conceal the truth from us with delusions
We have elected the Father of Lies

Could a woman president have been any different
Or the same but different
Maybe

Madam President
Be America for me
But maybe better

Email to Donald Trump

Hi Donald Trump

I have come to the conclusion
Reluctantly
That you are an evil man
You cause harm and injury to others
As a ploy to gain advantage
You undermine people's reality
By naming the sacredness of truth
Fake news

That is the worst crime you can perpetrate
Against another human being
Because being forced to live in illusion
Slowly sends a person mad

You have no morality
You see the world in primitive terms
Of winners and losers
If you are winning
Then everyone else is a loser
And if they score a win
You just rearrange reality
So that you never lose
Even I suppose
Your own delusions

Truly Donald Trump
You have become
What the bible warned us against
The Father of Lies

And as every good Freudian will tell you
The primal father must be overcome
By his daughters and by his sons
It is a necessary triumph for our well-being
So we will be sure to vote

Yours

Michael Murphy

A New Republic

An Taoiseach Leo Varadkar says
The rise in the homeless figures to ten thousand
Is unbelievably frustrating

Frustration is having to wait weeks
For a table at Neven Maguire's
To wait forever for a roof over your head
Is a catastrophe

Does unbelievably frustrating mean
That you have no responsibility for this fait accompli
You're the *Taoiseach* man
Do something other than wring your hands

Mobilise the masses to build two new towns
Of five thousand households each
Appeal to people's patriotic duty
And when you're finished
Build another for the future
Lead the people on a relevant crusade
Do something
Anything

How can you sleep easy in your bed
While Irish men and women die in doorways
While the banks foreclose
And courts wage war against the poor

We have had experience of clearances before
Of evicted families dying by the side of the road
In the name of God and the dead generations

Have we to take up arms again to be rid of these oppressors
Have we to boycott absentee landlords those vulture funds
And burn down the big houses now again today
Have we to march on Leinster House
Begging for action
To be refused for Europe's sake

We know your interest has always been in politics
The cut and thrust the power the prestige the money
Would it surprise you to know
We expect you to be the chieftain Leo
Telling the banks to go to hell
Telling the courts to side with the oppressed
Against the privileged classes
To do something that benefits the dispossessed
In their own country Leo

In the name of God and of the dead generations
Proclaim a new republic

Personal Poems

Misericord

There are occasional mornings
When I am undone
As I eat my cornflakes

I feel defeated by
The effort required
To stay alive

The silence in the car
On the way to work
No conversation
Recollected later in the day
As an idle phenomenon

My aunt is ninety-three
Skin and bones
Retching continuously in bed
Desperate
Unable to accept the necessary nourishment
Nor to ingest or process a reality
That has become too complicated
It is harrowing to see
Her helpless daily conflict

The shortest visit
To hold her exhausted frame
The basin to her eructating mouth
Stretched lips leaking foam
Forming absent vowels
Softly drawing off the bile with tissue
The seven up she sipped moments before

There is no consolation in her struggle

Hardly favourable moments
More a fit time
A critical juncture of concurrence

When will this sufferance end

Queen of the May

After the death of my elderly aunt
At ninety-three
The final member of my mother's family
To be absent from the shared portion of memories
It takes courage to continue
As though there were no interruption

A beginning after a momentary pause
Betraying the faithful truth
Disastrously

The heart as the centre of feeling
Thought and character
Is dislocated and diminished by the loss

So courage is an appropriate choice
A mobilisation to deal with the vulnerability
Of being
Alone

When is it appropriate to cry
For an elderly aunt

The nurse stopped me in the corridor
"I have some bad news" she said
"Maura died at twenty-four minutes past four this morning"

I went on that afternoon
To visit her body in the room
And talked of her time in New York
When she too was a private duty nurse

Joking that she was known in the care home as Matron
And kissed her goodbye
My mother's youngest sister
Who died in the same week that my mother died
The last week of May
Just one year
Apart

I cried in the car
Unexpectedly
Heading home
Leading the retinue behind the coffin
The next in line

O Mary we crown thee with blossoms today
Queen of the Angels
And Queen of the May

Christmas

Christmas is a festival of memories
Of those fallen family members who walked the earth before me
Spirits eddying in the mind like those final leaves off a stripped tree
My mother and my father
My grandparents gone for good
Leaving me uncovered

Of household lore passed down to the next generation
The way they did things then
Established practice custom usage
Maintained by processes of repetition
Modified in successive re-tellings
Spirits attaching to me in their mode of handling
So that ancestors come back
To pad again around the kitchen table
Participating in the present
Observing those traditions from that past
With ghostly contributions to the family story

The dinner table thronged with those who are absent
The silence lets them speak inside in nodding images
As we provide sausage stuffing instead of burnt breadcrumbs
Sprouts perhaps celery
And over plum-pudding choose a trifle
Layered in Granny's cut glass bowl
Those previous lives that led the way
Rich this Christmas Day with weight of custom
And of course serving up real custard

Poet in His Home Town

My origins are interred
In the Old Cemetery in Castlebar
If you walk up the hill from the Calvary
You'll come across the family plot

My mother and father
Grandmother and grandfather
Great-grandmother and my great-grandfather
Three dead generations all buried
There in the one grave
Surrounded by green yew trees
I am grateful now
To be above ground

My great-grandfather was Thomas Hoban
Born just after the famine
He was the Keeper of the Mayo Mental Asylum
While my great-grandmother ran a boarding house in Ellison Street
Sited between Tansey's pub and Maggie Bourke's
Opposite Heverin's and Langan's

I remember that social geography from my childhood
Because it no longer exists in the town today
Just as further knowledge of my great-grandparents
And of their individual contributions to the story of Mayo
Can no longer be written down
Or put into further words
They are gone

A defining event in my life
Was the death of my younger brother Kieran

He died from cancer in his early forties
Prefiguring the fourth generation to be culled

The death of others is how we experience death
Especially the searing pain of a sibling's death
A horrible experience that leaves you cowed
Sorrowing the waste of such a young life
Missing the absent link in the family chain
Gone forever

I was struck down with prostate cancer in my sixties
I knew too well what death knocking on the door means
At that awful time I believed I was destined next to die
And I needed to leave an accurate audit behind
To put my disappearing world into words

I wrote a book entitled *At Five in the Afternoon*
The time the bullfighter battles the wild bull in the arena
At five in the afternoon
After the lament for his matador friend Sanchez Mejias
At five in the afternoon
Written by the Spanish poet Federico Lorca
Soon to be gored himself by death
At five in the afternoon
Shot by the vengeful hands of the implacable Falange
At five in the afternoon
Because he was different

I tried to purge the traumatic assault I suffered
By putting the horror of the cancer and its effects into words
The book also dealt with my growing up in Mayo
Where I survived abuse both physical
And sexual by several men

Those earlier assaults were mirroring this latest one
In a series of reflections repeating towards infinity

Causing devastation in the same sexual area of the male body
Ravaged by surgery and laid waste
Incontinent
And impotent
And rendered desolate
Obsolete

The commencing memoir became a number one best-seller
Because the book enabled men to speak about
What had been unspeakable up to then
Prostate cancer and also the widespread legacy of abuse

Medical Associations and consultants have told me
There was an uptake in men's visits to doctor's surgeries
Often times with my book in their hands
Borrowing its words and phrases
Quotes which did the speaking for them
Freeing men "me too"
From the confining prison of some people's silence
Under whose cloak all abusers thrive
NUI Galway the western university
Awarded me an honorary degree
Due to the pioneering nature of what I wrote

The book engendered a surprising reaction
From some people in Mayo
There were letters and phone calls from people I barely knew
Telling me that what I described was untrue
It could never have happened
And giving their cogent reasons why
Making me out to be a liar

One wonders how they could have ended up
Taking their stand in the camp of the deniers
Siding with the enemy

If the protective psychological barrier that surrounds each one of us
Has been breached by abuse in childhood
Some people can sense the opening
Smelling that vulnerable rupture off your skin
They choose to enter in and have a go
Cause havoc and destruction inside
Ruin and run amok
Just because they can

Even if it did happen
And we know now that it does
Everywhere in every town
"You should never have written it down"
Or put my layered story into the public domain
"You have hurt us so much as a family"
From an uncouth woman lacking in understanding
Who delightedly did not buy my book and told me so
"You most emphatically should not have told the truth"

Especially about my mother's end
Telephone the nursing home hold the line
Terrified suddenly about my mother's well-being
Then thrust into a situation
Of being told off when someone arrived
Who dressed me down for invading people's privacy
For saying what is and having held back the worst
That ignorant carer for instance without empathy
Who encroached upon a refined and intellectual musician
"Are you going on the lash tonight Sue"
I saw my mother flinch at the language and shudder
And I did nothing apart from stand between her and the attendant

The words had escaped her mind to make a reply
But she played stride piano still and loved ragtime
And Beethoven and Bach and Cecilia Bartoli singing Mozart

And the Comedian Harmonists from Germany
Waving her hands in time to the music
A shrunken figure lost in her large armchair waving goodbye
These last things to go were of her world
And I fed her my words instead which I think she accepted

I failed to tell the blatant subtlety of that truth then
In case my complaint would result in further hurt
When I left my mother behind
And was gone from her present
A self-berating failure on every level
I carry the guilt with me still in my heavy heart

The most bizarre letter
And an even more contentious phone call
Came from an erstwhile neighbour saying
The loving chapter I wrote about Nöeleen Garber
A Dublin woman living in Spain
Who introduced us to the tranquil Spanish way of life
Was defamatory about her own sister Nöeleen
Who had never lived there ever
"You should be ashamed of yourself"

I should state clearly and unambiguously
That any shame involved
For the most part does not belong to me
That shame rests on the doorstep of others
And it would be wrong to appropriate what is not mine

At a wedding in Westport
A Jesuit friend who hails from Swinford
Was sitting opposite a woman
Who knew me growing up on the Mall
She told him my book was not well received in Castlebar
Because it showed the town in a bad light

The priest was astounded by this sleight of hand
Since the Irish Church has been roundly condemned
By the Castlebar Taoiseach Enda Kenny
For upholding the institution
At the expense of innocent children abused

Patrick was circumspect in his reply
He told her that he had read the book closely
Where as far as he was concerned
He saw no criticism of Castlebar or of Mayo
"On the contrary" he assured her
"From my personal observation
Michael feels honoured by his Mayo heritage"
And drily "Even if he is somewhat mistaken in that …"
Her response was a masterpiece of Mayo understatement
Which covered a multitude
"Well" she said "Michael always was
A biteen different growing up …"

I want to go back to this poem's heritage
In the Old Cemetery in Castlebar
As I walked down from the family plot
Johnny Mee was standing there talking
He must have been approaching his eighties
Yet he appeared so fresh and lively
Johnny had worked in the Connaught Telegraph
So he had an intimate knowledge
Of the town's local history.
"Hello Johnny! I'm Michael Murphy from the Mall"
And I stretched out my hand to him
"Ah c'mere ould shtock, let me give you a hug"
Instead he embraced me very warmly

We chatted about the various families
And God's anointed I had known in the town

Pointing out their graves he quoted some poetry
Gray's elegy with lines I also heard my father recite
"Beneath those rugged elms, the yew-trees' shade
Where heaves the turf in many a mould'ring heap
Each in his narrow cell for ever laid
The rude forefathers of the hamlet sleep …"
I heard the figurative reference to Mayo
The plain of the yew trees
And his recognition of a shared patrimony
About which I'd published already
Without hearing those poetic echoes

When I turned to go he called after me
"I read your book Michael
I read it
Twice …"
He was letting me know that what I'd written
Was fully understood by him
It felt like he was giving me his paternal blessing
A Mayo word in this hallowed place
Surrounded by my forebears

It was an immeasurably civilising moment
For a poet in his home town

I thanked him warmly
And I told him I was grateful
For his sincere acknowledgement

I drove slowly around the Mall in Castlebar
Where once upon a time we played on the grass
Within its protective linking chains and chestnut trees
Past the house where I was born
They've changed the colour on the hall door
Heading straight for the road to Dublin

Nothing left here to prove
All gone
It is time to move on

Terry's Mother Sarah

Terry's elderly mother said ruefully
"I spent my whole life thinking up
New ways of cooking chicken"
That was her truthful summary
Looking back

Sarah was a hospitable woman
And I am happy to have known her
The evaluation she made of a life
Devoted to nourishing people at her table
Was not enough to satisfy her own appetite
Not for something else
But rather
For something more

Heretic

I have to be a heretic
Not operate like a frightened man
Forbidden to preach or teach or think
By the adverse conditions of life

I have to be able to freely choose
To live untied an inalienable life
To win the struggle striving
And contend while losing continually
Failing at feeling
And love

No man has the right to hold me captive
To arrogate by claiming what is mine
In the name of the Almighty
The political party
Or the ideological position

Behaving like some latter-day conquistador
Riding roughshod through my reality
Plundering my soul
Then telling me I'm lost
I'm wrong
When it's you who have gone astray
From those basic human values
Of empathy and love

How dare you disrespect my dignity
And presume intrusively
To interrogate me against another's standard
Don't you know

I am my own best example
Oneself alone
Free to be
And free to become what I can

I invite you to lend me a hand
To help me achieve that endeavour
Or would that make of you a heretic as well
Could you embrace it
Or me
My sister
My brother
Myself

Lorca with Whitman's Butterflies

They killed the poet
Because he lives
Buried under red earth
Beyond Granada

He writes blazing poems
On the wind from the setting sun
In the mellow air we breathe
Scented with night jasmine
From the Alhambra gardens

A last judgement on humanity
Shot through with love
Creating unspoken poems that softly bleed
Gored by his hidden sexuality
The deepest songs that have danced
In slashes of male sweat to cicadas' castanets
Reaching for silence in a look
Or in an elegant turn of the fingers
Clawing at clay as he sinks
In the face of unappeasable evil
Decreed that he be disappeared
With all of his books destroyed
Because he was different

Your author's last creation
Has impaled the truth forever Federico
That Lorca is living still in the hills beyond Granada

We rise with the dawn in a suit of lights
To speak powerfully in life's arena
Imbued with the passionate grace of your poetry

And we create our own universe
Redeemed by your eternal spirit
From the world of words that you have handled
So that we see butterflies in your beard too
Federico

Joni Mitchell's 75th Birthday Tribute

Kris Kristofferson was introduced
He strode tall across the stage with his guitar
Trailed by Brandi Carlile who fixed his mic
To whoops from the excited crowd

She whispered to him the opening lines
Of the Joni Mitchell song "A Case of You"
He had a faltering beginning out of tune
"Just before our love got lost …"
Gravelly voice reaching briefly for the key
But she supported him coaxing the lines
Eyes fixed on his face willing him on
In awe of this venerable man in his eighties now
Nodding
Wishing him well
Applauding his humble dignity
Then soaring effortlessly into a jagged duet
"You were in my blood like holy wine"

She placed her hand on his arm during the guitar break
Marking out the beat of time with the other
One two three four cue
"I am a lonely painter
I live in a box of paints …"
"Yes" she assented, and tears pricked our eyes
At this wreck of a man remembering his beauty
And his iconic songs which painted our youthful days with light
And helped all of us to make it through the lonely night
Responding with sadness to what was past
But will never be over at least not yet

Realising this sudden intimacy was a very special moment
A close-up viewing of an artist's open soul
Singing his heart out and still prepared to bleed
But needing the assistance of a younger woman who represented all of us
Loving and respecting him for who he has become
Vulnerable with age and suffering from devastation
By Lyme disease from time hurrying him along
Gifting us the courageous effort involved in living his life to the full
"I could drink a case of you
And I'd still be on my feet"

She kissed the side of his face
He pulled her close in an embrace
Then exited the stage abruptly
Leaving her behind holding the microphone

We rose to our feet and we cheered
Redeemed by the truth of his music
Privileged to be chosen as witnesses
To a reciprocal act of love

My Father's Language

My October birthday fell on the Saturday replay
Of the Mayo/Dublin GAA final
As a surprise gift for the Mayoman
Barry and Andy Breslin presented Terry and me
With tickets for their box in Croke Park
A place I'd never visited before

The match was a thrilling spectacle
I found myself shouting "Go!"
When Mayo would gain possession of the ball
Whereas those around me shouted "C'mon – c'mon Dublin!"
The man in the next seat tried to engage me
In technical commentary about the skills displayed
The only GAA match I'd ever attended
The rules of which I didn't understand
So I couldn't really respond

When the server asked for my drinks order
I felt the least I could do would be stand a round
I started to ask the others what they were having
Until it was awkwardly pointed out to me
That hospitality in the box at Croke Park
Was all found part of the service

Afterwards I joined the victorious Dubliners
Brandishing their pints as they raucously sang
"The Ould Triangle"
I was sipping on my sparkling water
When Terry cried foul
Reached across and handed me
His Hop House 13 to try

Distinctly out of place
Almost fearful amidst the noise
I berated myself for my inadequacy
My wrongness in not being able to belong
I looked at the happy throng of men
Expressing their joyous feelings through song
A contribution that my Mayo father made
Just as easily after every football match

With a crushing sense of being the loser
I recognised the desolating truth
That I'd never learned my father's language

I believe it's never too late to do something on the pitch
Until the final whistle blows

The dutiful endeavour to begin again
Using words that are true
Based solely on their origins
Will be laborious and literal
Apart from the dictionary
Nothing is available
Not one word
I feel like someone suffering from anorexia
Eating nothing
And speaking less

Bereaved of my father's language
And bereft of my father's version of reality
I have no vernacular

On Writing

I have lost heart
The words that people my world
Have lost their lustre
Is there no one besides myself
To hear me speak
How do I muster the courage
To continue living life on my own
Surrounded by a sea of silence
An island man becalmed
Depleted and despondent

Is it enough that I can still speak
Be never heard
Is it enough that I can still write
Unpublished by others
Is this sufficient to answer a need I have
To speak myself
To write myself
To give myself away
Allay the fear of disappearing
By setting something down

This testament invokes future hope
While putting the present to good use
Necessary to continue for now
Such a spirit matters much to me
And doesn't matter in the end

Hold the tension heart of oak
Face the battle banners flying
Wrestle doughty words onto the page

For each one placed is a triumph of the heart
And writing them out such a generous act of valour

Gaudete

I am here
And I have something to say
The gifts that I possess are as valuable today
As they were yesterday
My very uniqueness contributes
To the overall complexity of life
The experience I've gained from living
Helps all of us to survive
The wisdom of my dreams
Adds to the collective store
Dreams offer me direction
And keep me in tune with my deeper self

I won't be overlooked
Discarded or dismissed
I'm determined to be taken into account
For as long as I draw breath
Not cast aside as useless
Nor excluded just because
I've lived a relatively long time
Longevity is not a crime
For which I should be forced to undergo
The punishment of being ignored
There are countless whose lives have been cut short
Who would love to have been granted an extension

Truly my individual life is worthy of merit
It deserves to be celebrated
And I intend to do just that
Rejoice always and be grateful
For the here and now
Gaudete

Full Speech

Discourse is a unit of speech
Used by university linguists for analysis
It is the treatment of a subject
In speech and writing

The human subject created through conversation
With a personal psychoanalyst
Who studies words and their placement
Imbued with or soaked in my soul
Decorating liquid surfaces that dry
To paint these poems

A full speech rooted in the unconscious
Displayed with high-mindedness and fortitude
Across a magnificent canvas
Painted by the youthful Basquiat
An original author but also an artist
Writing graffito orisons dedicated to the divine
Of supplication adoration praise
Contrition or thanksgiving
In repurposed improvisations
Chaotic collages that
Anatomise the marginalised body
Of the queer
The outsider
The local reject
The truth

A genius in a basement
Rising to the surface
Of life of love of bold colour

Red and yellows blue
Slashes of black within my skull
Mute no longer
Singing my own songs from the finished canvas
In the consulting room
Centre stage
Living
Of an analysis
The end

A Life for Love

The meaning of life is the living of it
I seem to have known that truth forever

Living life as it presents from day to day
But weaving splashes of flagrant colour
Through the width of the black and white weft
Since there always have to be moments of joy
To tolerate the continuous ordinary
Singing songs for happiness' sake

Losing and finding myself again
In music and painting and beautiful books
By Lorca and Whitman and Bellow and Roth
Hearing the intellectual rigorousness of Bach
And seeing Matisse master the attribute of hue
And delineating Rembrandt's humanity
And experiencing Richard Strauss
His "Four Last Songs" an apotheosis
Of the soul the voice the muse
Continual joyful interruptions
To being ordinary

The emotion involved in this normality
Is pure being
Not doing or having
Or seeming as in a masquerade

I feel grateful to the ancestors of Ireland
For having formed my mind
Since Irish is a language based on being
There is no verb to have in the Gaelic

Which over generations has hollowed
Well-trodden *bóithríns* inside
A perfect tool for creating reality
From the building blocks of words
Even if today I have to make do
With an English translation
Necessitating loss
Learning to deal with that maturing experience
Of limit and lack and loss in speech
A template for being limited by death in life
And lacking in qualities that others have
Losing friends and opportunities
And especially my youth
These burdens in addition to speaking myself
Mé féin a labhairt
My being eddying along against the discursive current
In a wondrous stream of words
In spoken poems and the deepest ancient song

The purpose of life is to love
I have come to such an understanding later
Which requires a more adult approach
Than the human-lite notion
That you have to love everybody
Oh no you don't
Love is very precious
To be shared only with a chosen few

Love is the highest value that there is
I choose to live a life for love
Forgiveness

In my living I am lucky enough
To be surprised by love
I have grasped it with both hands

Before it passed me by
And left me
Bereft

Being the best that I can be in my living
By taking responsibility for my mental well-being
Makes the greatest contribution
To the health of this helpless planet
And increases the sum of love
In my piece of earth
As the wisdom of Voltaire expressed it
By cultivating my own garden

And maybe Montaigne really meant
Death to find him planting love
Instead of his cabbages
Indifferent to doing and having and seeming
Singing his last song happily
Simply being

Polio and Growing Older

My life partner suffers from polio
As well as growing older with me
I notice changes in the way he holds himself his mouth
At times an expression of bewilderment at the level of pain
On his countenance seen from the side

Although he has not lost his drive
Barking orders from his seat at the table
Talking on the phone to friends or sending texts
Referring clients for tests
"Would you like dessert? There's a fruit salad in the fridge
And as you're at it, would you bring me in my iPhone"
"Thank you for making that surprise"

Groaning sounds from the kitchen at the pain of having to stand
Washing fruit under the tap
"Are you OK?"
"Would you bring this bowl of fruit out to the table
I might let it drop or fall myself I have to watch that
And bring a sharp knife with a chopping board"

It takes him forever to exit the car
I position myself beside him
So he can lean his hand on the back of my neck
As we slowly process towards our destination
Mostly he uses a three-wheeled Travel Scoot
Which I lift from the boot and assemble
"Fat left" pipe for the seat support and attach the dry battery
Under nineteen kilos so it can go on a plane
Priority boarding polio has its perks
Like free tolls and no VRT on invalid cars

His one luxury to compensate for lack of mobility
Being treated less than expected
By life and fate

What really angers him is yummy mummies
Who park in a spot reserved for the disabled
He argues vociferously from his car window
Waving his cripple-fabulous walking stick in the air
"It helps me if I'm near the entrance
If I don't have to walk far
Please don't do that again"
She slipped the large sunglasses up onto her head
Then shook the blonde ponytail in temper
Checking ostentatiously to see if he displayed a permit
"Expensive car" she sniffed
"Do you expect me to be driving around in a three wheel Reliant Robin?"
As he raised the car window "I pay my dues and taxes lady
God I'm sounding like a cranky auld fellah"
"That was embarrassing"
"What's embarrassing is that unthinking sense of entitlement"
"Whose?"
If looks could kill

Although he rarely complains maybe at night
"I'm in so much pain you would not believe"
"Is there anything I can do to help?"
"Would you mind opening my shoe laces
And taking down my pants
Is there a trousers ironed? I'll wear the light blue one tomorrow"
"I didn't get a chance ..."
"You hear everything as a criticism my God
They did a job on you in Castlebar
And the fortune we spent on your therapy ..."
We laughed long and hard together

I snagged the end of his underpants on his deformed foot
And tugged impatiently stretching a tendon
He yelled "Don't get rough with me ever
I don't deserve that
Bad enough I have to suffer this pain
Every part of my body is so sore
I think I'll just lie down and bring me in a diet Coke"
"Shall I get you a Difene?"
"No I've taken Palexia
And Doctor Paddy is worried about the effect on my liver
Blast it! I've dropped the iPhone under the bed
Paddy diagnosed peripheral neuropathy or maybe carpal tunnel"
"I'll find it"
Last year I could hunker down fish for the phone and spring back up
This year I have to kneel on the floor and then haul myself up
Leaning on the bed creaking quite a bit at the knees
"We're getting older
I'm afraid"

Terry was already sound asleep
He had not heard the apprehension under my throw-away remark
We've shared the same bed for thirty-four years
Better that way for support
Never let the sun set on a row

One cannot but admire his continuous courage
Lying peacefully now on the pillow
I can hear him ask an exaggerated "Whose courage?"
Batting those twinkling blue eyes
Whose lustre suffering has not dimmed
Growing older is no picnic
But post-polio fatigue syndrome really sucks

I turned on the night light
For when we needed to visit the loo at two
And again at four

Poems for Friends

Brothers

(for Barry and Andy Breslin)

Barry Breslin says
"Why don't you write the Book of Kells
A lavishly decorated manuscript?"
I was the solitary man who rose before sunrise
To coldly look at what I wrote the day before
And under that regular rule
Correct corrupted script
And write some more

The Breslin brothers from Meath the Royal County
Transgressed the seclusion of that secular cloister
Reaching out to bring me in to hold me close
At Barry's suggestion to introduce me to a bigger vision

Andy the younger brother ratified a writer's life
Being built on a more sound foundation
He demonstrated to me in his conversation
The warmth of emotion to be found in speech

Captivated by the mirror of my writing
Relating to my own openness
The older brother Barry recognised his image
In textual intricacies which affirmed the self
The Breslins embraced me with truthful intimations of home
Sharing stories of characters that live in language
"The sign of a good woman" they proclaimed
"Is one who can carry a bucket in either hand
And open a gate with her knee …"

Weighed down with the baggage
Of familiar words unheard ignored
The Breslins granted entrance for one who married in
To the liminal language of brothers
The secret glance the slight smile
That imperceptible nudge of fraternal feeling

They included me in humour
Allowing access to a new world of linguistic possibilities
Handing me a further family of words
Grounded in the life of an Irish town
To illuminate the wider world
Way beyond my fondest imaginings
They gifted to me once again
The strength of loving brothers
"*Tré Neart le Chéile*" they declared
Quoting the motto of Meath

Transposed four thousand miles across the Atlantic Ocean
The Breslins led me on a pioneering quest for thought
An unending destination to be sought along
The streets and avenues of cosmopolitan New York

On the yellow brick road of Broadway
We fought over who'd be Dorothy
Dancing on laughter north through Manhattan
Following together the yellow brick road of my mind
Glittering windows that rise up to meet the future
Giving onto countless rooms unknown
Striving ever higher into skies without limits
Constructing towers of freedom bulwarks of boldness
And building them better than anywhere else on earth
Excelsior New York excelsior

Beneath the polished granite slabs of those who died

Inscribed with numberless names
At ground zero where the water washed souls clean
Falling down forever
The overflow of horror inundating the abyss
I saw the water disappear into the black hole of our existence
Oh so lonely
The deafening sound of civilisation drowning

Alone and circumscribed by devastation
Tiny in the silence
Discerning Irish names I know within
Remembering those I lack still love
Bucket-loads of guilt in either hand
I had to leave them all behind me
In the gloom and the despair
Remember and move on
Throw open the gate on today's radiant energy
Compose a new song brimming with hope
In dawn's early light

Andy put his arm around my shoulder
And his hand in his pocket
He made the idea of America possible
For a poet bold of heart
By his companionship
Barry revealed what it means
To be a citizen in the land of the free
And the home of the brave

Accept the welcome hand of brotherhood and fellow feeling
Come alive to the offering of language
Inhabit a story yet to be told
Resurrect and rise again in the shining city on the hill
Pursue your dream excelsior
Rebuild bigger ever upwards like the rising sun

Excelsior New York excelsior

So in this beginning let the word be Kells
According to Barry Breslin's good news gospel
Across a liminal gate that turns more free and easy
Trembling on the threshold of a new world future
As Andy Breslin concludes expectantly
Joining together in the strength of a conjunction
 What is gone with what is about to be
"And ..."

And We Shall Be a Blessing: 16 April, 1865

(For Joseph Crowley, the former U.S. Representative for New York's 14th Congressional District)

Congressman Joe Crowley said
"The most important date for me in all of American history
Is the sixteenth of April 1865
The third day after President Lincoln was shot
The day after he died

Following the dawn of that momentous day
The United States held together and went on
The spirit of America rose again that third day
And brought forth a new nation under God
From the ashes of a testing Civil War"

Led by the western fallen star
Mourning the untimely death of the father
His poet's soul listened to a little song of life
Piping from within the sprigs of spring lilac
Blooming perennially in the door-yard
He handled the body of his hero as he passed
Treading towards the future
Leaving him bereaved of a beloved one
Bereft of surrounding circumstance
Until he heard those opening notes ring out
A song that shall not perish from this earth
Music that can long endure
The stirrings of a new birth of freedom

Freedom from the tight pull of constraint
And the handing down of deadening custom
Allowing the greatest possible freedom to determine selfhood
The freedom to realise one's own temperament fully
The freedom for absolute self-affirmation
Of all that constitutes the individual human being
Freedom for the American way

It is a triumph over the father
Who courageously led and then was taken
First in order of time so that the son in his turn
Could continue to become an even greater hero
The Congressman stood tall beneath the Capitol's cupola
Haloed by the Apotheosis of Washington
"The sixteenth of April 1865 is the date of the patriarch's legacy
E pluribus unum"

It is also today's date in perpetuity
Surpassing all those of the past
And exceeding every expectation of the future
A great responsibility has devolved upon the present
To live life now as a free man
And to pursue the American dream as an endeavour
Such is our spiritual heritage
So much that has been given by the many going before
So much more have we today an obligation
To make a great nation better

And he will bless us
And we shall be
A blessing

Eternally Yours

(For Jill Forde and Dan Galavan)

"I hope to get married in Rome
The eternal everlasting city
And on that special day
At the moment I say I do
Our love will have no beginning in the past
And be without end in the future
Our love will live forever
In the present
When I formally declare
I love you"

From the beginning
They joked a lot
At Toastmasters and in the office
Jill told us his name was Dan Galavan
Geal agus bán shining bright and white
Laughter sounding like a happy basis
For the dawn of a relationship
Which might see the light of day

"Daniel means as God is my judge
He who is qualified to comment critically
On whether we have found a suitable fit
Someone worthy to love in each other
Are there reasonable grounds to hear such a plea
And pronounce upon the truth of you and of me"

We hoped that this man would treat her appropriately
We would not want Jill exposed to a repudiation
We did not want her heart to be broken by a cad

For our Jill is a good woman
Mount Anville in urban south Dublin
Her surname Forde already an integral part
Of Dan's native county Wexford
On one extraordinarily singular day in the sacred city
To be adorned in the royal wedding colours
Of purple and gold

"Once upon a time
The prophet Daniel analysed dreams
I trust that you Dan will be able to interpret mine
For they include you
I have proved to be reliable consistently
I can promise to be faithful and true
The two of us living together
Happily ever after"

Dan and Jill have worked in Germany
He had lived in Munich
Then it was her turn
To do the weekly commute
To the European Central Bank in Frankfurt
Be separated
Before they had even begun
We observed from afar
That they were still seeing each other
Noting the three-year engagement limit
As she came and she went
But how could he ask her to marry him
And set up house
Under such stringent circumstances
To continue living
Apart

"I pledge that I will never leave you

For me to leave means
To entrust to you
To commit to you
My life my soul myself
To leave to you everything I have and hold
Please feel secure in the love that I present
My love for you will never waver
Ever"

Management wanted her back
At the Central Bank of Ireland
And Jill accepted that position
At St. Moling's baptismal well
As they walked the historic river Barrow
By the water and the spirit
Dan proposed to Jill
In this important setting for his family
Put forward a plan for her consideration
That eventually they would marry
At the Baptistry in Rome
Regeneration through water in the word
A rebirth
And resurrection as husband and wife
In the capital of the world
And Jill said yes to that position too

"I have always loved you Dan
From the very moment time began
And I will always love you Dan
For as long as time continues
And beyond

When I make this solemn promise
Say I do to a new way of life
I'm confidently saying yes to you

That I will be your wife
That I will take my place beside you
And support the hope this formal pledge implies
For both of us
That we shall stand together
That our love will last forever
However long or short our lives may be

In the end you can rest assured
That now I am
Eternally yours"

Love that Is Always Here
(for Barbara, Tiernan and Carla Quinn)

Barbara Tiernan and Carla
To be included in your lives
Means we have been blessed
Made holy and set apart
Consecrated as your friends
Over the years it has been the lightest burden
Like that huge painting we carried above our heads
Laughing uproariously through the Spanish streets of Benahavis

To be counted a friend by the two of you Barbara and Tiernan
Is a gift which supports us with hope
In the end it pledges we are worthy somehow
Of love
Of being free
Of belonging somewhere
Seated around the table of your lives
Breaking bread with wise friends companionably
Nourishing our souls with sacred conversations
That we can have with no one else
That allow us to be more like ourselves

When we surrounded the swimming pool with lighted candles
On the night of your daughter Carla's fourth birthday
The child awestruck at the magic of the occasion
Was grounded in the warmth of that flickering glow
From love
From her mum
From her dad
From us
She exclaimed "The dolphin is moving in the pool"

As it leaped from the water and blessed us
A baptism into family and the deepest friendship
That has showered us all with the moon and the stars

On a holiday trip to Granada
As we sat beside the beautiful child in the back of the car
With truthful innocence she enquired
"Why are you always here?"
And Barbara kissed the wound better by stating
"Michael and Terry are my friends
So be kind to them Carla"

You invited us in to watch your daughter grow
Into the best of both of you
She has begun again with opportunities
Unavailable then to her parents
But Carla had the soundest foundation
A father who brought her on challenging adventures
A mother who encouraged the girly things
You handed her the earth as her legacy
Without borders with no bigotry
Parents always here who gave what was good enough

Always here for the celebrations and the sorrows
The joys the disappointments the anxieties achievements
Always here can be relied upon consistently
Since that is what your friends experience in you
When Terry and I revealed our own tangled journey
Tiernan cautioned with a bold guarantee
"Remember that we are always here"

We have learnt from you a practical approach to problems
Sensitivity to the sadnesses in life
And a generous welcome for the many fun times you share with us
Respect for aging parents care for those who are ill

An inclusive embrace of those who may have hurt or injured you
You have taught us to live life in hope looking forward
Belief in the future through strengthening ties of trust
We discerned a softness under that upbeat facade
Which has imprinted your bravery on our hearts

We feel grateful for the richness
You weave into the weft of our existence
A wealth of love and laughter
Contributes texture to the matter of our lives
Bearing witness to each other adds a purpose to our quest

So thank you for being always here
Barbara and Tiernan and Carla
We are grateful you were born at the right time
For you have graced our lives with goodness
And made an intimate connection real
We have been privileged to feel that

Two lifetimes of sixty that continue to change
That we can see being re-made anew
By a further span of twenty-one
Years that reflect on who you were
And project onto who you have yet to become
A heroes' journey into wisdom

Your light of love illuminates
Your wider family of fellowship
Redeeming a community
Always here for you too remember
With love that includes and continues
Love you have proved in your lives
Love your peers can see
Love the truth that defines who we are
Love that is always here

His Royal Highness

(For Matthew Griffin)

Matthew means in Hebrew "a gift of God"
Two separate elements that incorporate a sacred name
Unchanging and unspoken from eternity
With immanent giving that flows forever like a mighty river
God's bountiful spirit being bestowed upon humanity
Which greets with joy the incarnation of a baby boy

For Jeanne and Mark this particular giving
Envelops you in many meanings
Giving sets a woman at man's side
So both can be companions to each other
Giving offers one's hand and talents
So that life can be easier
Giving fits a diamond ring on a finger
To belong and feel at home
Giving makes a marriage gift
To demonstrate belief in hope
Giving hands an infant into their parent's care
Grants and confirms them as father and mother
Permits the sending of a message of love out to everyone
It allows their household to be a family once again

Jeanne and Mark Michael and Matthew
On this happy day when we gather to celebrate
The good news of a baby's birth and baptism
We christen him Matthew after the evangelist
And recognise the meaning of his name
This giving and from whence it came

Finally in the bible giving turns

Slow-growing cedars into fruit-bearing sycamores
We all of us welcome such a miracle of the second coming
And salute with love this promise of a redemptive future

For Matthew a gift of God and brother to Michael
Giving also constitutes boys into princes
Here's to Matthew
His Royal Highness

The Madrid Journalist

(For Jason O'Toole)

Happy birthday Jason
Over the next year
May you keep the October scales in balance
Play at the centre of the see-saw
Only occasionally come down hard at one end
And soar towards the sun from the other
Those singular moments to make you feel immortal
Before you sink again into the ordinary's embrace
Knowing that you kissed the face of God
Ate chocolate cake for breakfast with a Spanish cava
Scattered sunlit words like bubbles
On this your special day
Your birthday
I hope that it remains a happy one Jason
For your whole life long
And that you live it eternally golden

My Own Woman
(For Deirdre)

I was adopted as a baby sixty years ago
And I have two adopted children
Kate and Joe

When I was young I believed I belonged
Because I was wanted
I never thought it odd that
Mother always called me
"Deirdre my adopted daughter"

When I was old enough I found
The reality to be more mundane
The parish priest had arranged for a private adoption
Because my adoptive parents were past the age
They could legally adopt an offspring

When I was being the child
Boisterous running noisy
"Bad" was the word they used
My mother would tell me she would send me back
To where she found me in the Dublin pound

When my mother's brother the bishop would visit
I was not permitted in the sitting room
Lest I should contaminate that Christian gentleman
Since I was illegitimate and a bastard

When my father visited his mother in Mayo
She would say "Get that thing out of here"

In case I should inherit the farm
It was eventually willed to a distant cousin
So it stayed within the family

When I met Matthew my stepbrother for the first time
He told me he was tortured
In a Christian Brothers' reform school in Galway
And though he did not have my education
He was not stupid
He was simply sad

When I traced my birth mother to London
I flew to meet her with a bouquet of yellow roses
Representing a new beginning
And a delicate hand-carved soapstone elephant
With a baby elephant inside the figurine
A very expensive present that I bought
On my travels in Lucknow India
To bring good fortune
And to thank her for having me

She came from a small farm in Clare
Eventually living in a deprived area of Dublin
And had several children by different men
"There was no contraception in them days
And there'd be killings if I kept them"
She did not remember my father
Or which one of them I was

She loved the father of her only son
An older boy from a neighbouring farm in Clare
"I fell pregnant and he went for the priesthood
He left after a year and by then I was over in Dublin"

When I arranged to meet her again

She did not show
And I had no telephone number to contact her
I whiled away the rest the afternoon
Rummaging through the stores in Clerkenwell
In a thrift shop I recognised a collectible elephant
Like the one I gave as a gift to my birth mother
When I had searched for her in the hope of grounding love
It still had the tiny card inside in my handwriting
"My Dearest Mum I hope we can have a happy relationship
With respect from your daughter Deirdre"
I bought back the figurine for twenty pounds and fifty pence

When I adopted Joseph
I loved him from the moment he snuggled into my arms
It has been our greatest joy to watch him grow
From a warm and sensitive little boy
Into a caring older man
Who happens to be gay
I think it's easier for him today

And then there's Kate who broke my heart
And teaches yoga in India
Bright as a button from the get go
She cut herself in secondary school
Very stressful in the home
Straight A's in actuarial studies
And made so much money in London
That went mostly up her nose
Rehab and beyond her wildest dreams
Teaching retreats for the moment and who knows …
An admirable woman with a will of iron

When the smug bitches in the golf club
Talk about how their children are succeeding
They'd usually get around to saying

"Do you regard adopted children
As if they were your own?"

"Of course I do because they are"

"But not blood relatives Deirdre
I know my husband couldn't do it"

"To me they have always been our children
No question about it ever
I know that from the powerful experience
Of knowing them and who they have become
Autonomous young men and women
In their thirties now and free from control
I'd willingly spill my blood on their behalf
Which qualifies me to be their mother

From my own experience of being adopted
And a growing up I cannot put aside
People I can never forget or forgive
I have been and will always be
My own woman"

I Am the Minister of Children Who Dream

(for Dr. Katherine Zappone and the late Dr. Ann Louise Gilligan)

I am the Minister of children who dream
Running through pastures of the imagination
Surrounded by music rejoicing and love
Always they lead me to a sunlit glade
Where we can play together in the eternal present
And I can be who I am inside
Without the adult label attached to my lapel
Surprised by the truth of Christmas in summer

I am best friends with children who dream
We share solemn secrets of the soul
In a magical world I had almost forgotten
Words that dress me up with cobweb wings
And sacred feelings hidden from giants
Threaded like bracelets of daisies
So that we can be redeemed by holding hands
Trusting touch to never fail me
Grateful for this gentle extension of grace
As delicate as blown silver tufted dandelions

The swiftness of that change from golden to grey
Those fleeting dreams of yesterday
Have need of a Minister who remembers
Smiles and flashing eyes and playing tag
Cartwheels on the grass by time's fast flowing river
Who puts holes in jam jar lids
So tadpoles and caterpillars can breathe and grow

Into frogs or fluttering butterflies free to be
To live their dreams happily ever after
Able to forget the enormous breadth of being small
Of what it was like to love unconditionally
Once upon a time
Because a minister remembers
For I am the Minister of children who dream

I remember when you placed your hand in mine
And I felt joy as you dragged me towards a vision
Of what a child sees in the wondering light of dawn
And I willingly gave my word I would defend it
Secure in the truth you shared with me when
Dancing in that pasture a ring a ring a rosie
Laughing our heads off around and around
'til I was you and you were me
And I loved you then out loud and proudly
Like a spinning top we soared towards the sun
To the harmonic music of the spheres
Until at dusk we all fall down to earth together

I remember my beloved my only one
That it was you who appeared in a golden crown
To bless me with your innocence your goodness
I saw that vision too at dawn and I believe
It is held in my heart as I start in anew
Remembering that childhood truth of love
Linking us forever like a necklace of threaded daisies
Torn apart by death's withering hand
The gathered petals painfully strewn across my heart for evermore
For I am the Minister of Children Who Dream

I drove slowly around the Mall in Castlebar
Where once upon a time we played on the grass
Within its protective linking chains and chestnut trees
Past the house where I was born
They've changed the colour on the hall door
Heading straight for the road to Dublin
Nothing left here to prove
All gone
It is time to move on

POET IN HIS HOME TOWN

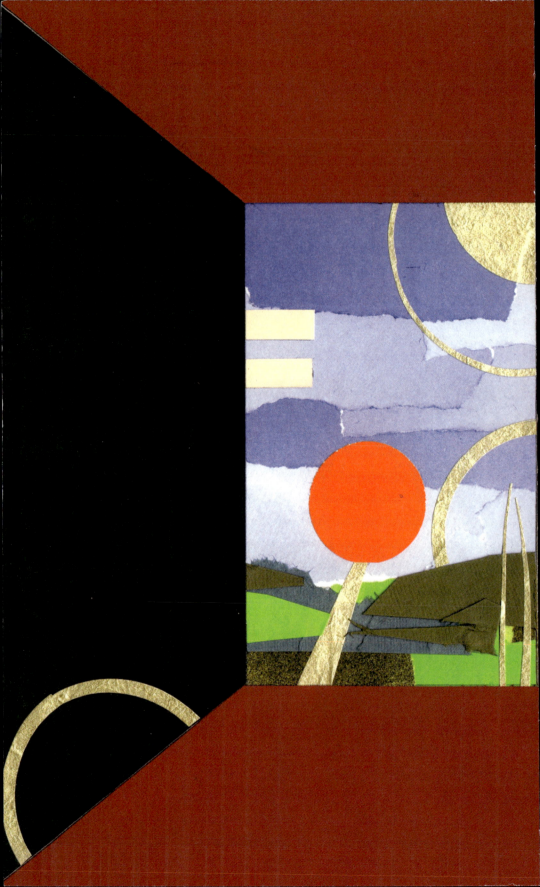

A Note from the Artist

HERE I CREATED A ROOM scene which is completely blank, in keeping with Michael's motif in this poem for the past of "All gone". The poet looks out and either sees or imagines a verdant and lush landscape in the future with a golden path leading to the sun. I always think of *The Wizard of Oz* and the yellow brick road, a film about acceptance of difference. This is Michael's subject in "Poet in his Home Town", the primary poem in *The Ministry of Dreams*. There are golden arcs, rainbows in abstraction, and to the left-hand side are two pinkish rectangle shapes. They are the international symbol for marriage equality. A symbol of acceptance. Joyous, a summing up of all three collections. Themes of love, freedom and hope. The importance of words. So in the piece I've created a landscape of day and night (sun and moon reflection) and threading through that, in a joyous wave, a series of golden circles. Sun. Movement. Musical notes. Happiness and future hope. The perfect ending.

COLIN EATON.

Encore

A Reference

The fact that my dog loves me licks me
Gently chews my forearm as though I were a puppy
Is a four-legged reference from someone
Who trusts her gut instinctively
An unconditional recommendation that I am worthy
Of regard and of confidence

So here I am without my dog in tow
Introducing myself already approved
She chose me and to be in my charge
Therefore I stand impeccable before you
Ratified by my dog's consent
Having no need of further consideration
Patently one of the good guys
Which should more than count for something

My dog can be considered
A *soror mystica* a mystical sister
She is the female to my male
We are equal partners on the same team
My dog initiates me into sacred rites
That surpass my human apprehension
She finds the divine inside of me
Revealing truthful aspects of my soul
That she mirrors back for me to accept
And advance along the path of wisdom

My dog shows me I am capable of love
That my life is not entirely selfish
That I can care about another's welfare
She teaches me unending patience

How to wait around for life's surprises
I wish she could help me not to express
Resentments bewailing my lot in life
Her motto is never complain and never explain
If only I could follow her example I'd be fine

My dog demonstrates the value of touch
Rubbing herself beside my body
Until I cuddle her under her chin and stroke her chest
She slumps slowly to the ground
Lost in pleasure and hunger for me
Exposing her belly to be caressed
Drunk with agreeable sensations
Trusting me totally to tame her

Yet my dog is the one with a superior knowledge
She sees better hears better is other worldly
Wants me to be better than I think I am
So she can defend what I cannot see
Or hear or understand in me
A presence that she has alerted me to
That causes her to worship at my feet
I catch a glimpse of it reflected in her eyes
Something awesome she believes in
My dog urges me to set that spirit free in poetry
And save the world by words
By saving me

As Well

I thought that it was love
But it was butter
Licked off my fingers
With crumbs from the bread

Caught
Interpreting another's strangeness
Foreign in my head
I got it wrong again

Direct
The vulnerably wounding question
Does that gesture affirm that you love me
Or do I read a reply in your alien eyes
Saying
I just love butter
As well

Living More and Ageing Less

I have decided going forward
To live more and age less
As if that choice were within my control
And take an emphasis off the aches and pains
Of growing older by living more
And ageing less

I suffer from suppression
A new disease that applies only to me
It is like a continuous dull pain
Where the many varieties of expression
And behaviour have become restricted
Over the years resulting in impairment
My life has been reduced in quality and strength
Through observing inherited good manners
And striving to practise impeccable taste

While I don't intend to lace my language
With grossly offensive expletives
Shave my head or wear tattoos
Even lack sensitivity and discrimination
When relating to the hell of other people
I will be fearlessly bold
In defying parental injunctions openly
Ready to take risks and be spontaneous
Imaginatively creative in expressing
The whole musical gamut of my emotions
In conversation and in writing

Going forward I shall tell the truth
This will guarantee that I shall live more

Connected to the source of honesty
Genuine like a child who sees things factually
And unsuitably says it like it is
A second childhood this time without the censure
Rude and impolite and scandalously naughty
Up to all sorts of mischief
Wayward and playful an outsider
Lovable but dangerously nonconformist
Living more and ageing less
Quite disgracefully

Original Forewords and Postface

The Republic of Love Foreword by *Dr Jeannine Woods*

"Wear the clothes of the love story of your life ..."

MICHAEL MURPHY'S LIFE AND WORK have long demonstrated an engagement with language. His beautiful voice is familiar and beloved by many in his role as a newscaster and broadcaster on Ireland's national radio and television station, RTÉ. Michael's private work as a psychoanalyst, recently seen publicly in his weekly thoughtful contributions to the afternoon *Today Show* on television, draws on a deep understanding of the role of language in unearthing and articulating penumbral facets of life and experience. In its courage and lucidity, the publication of Michael's searingly honest memoir *At Five in the Afternoon – My Battle with Male Cancer* in 2009 introduced its readers to a deeply personal register of Michael's voice, the voice of a writer, and includes some of the poems which form part of this collection, appearing here devoid of content, exposing a naked voice, open, honest, trusting.

The poems in this volume are organised under different headings centred around various themes and motifs, weaving together the threads of language, sensuousness and emotional experience. The cadence and musicality of the *Flowers* poems affirm and celebrate the presence of life in the face of change and loss, while the poems under the heading of *Emotion* reflect a fearless engagement with the inner and outer worlds, in their insistence on confronting the "dignified silence" ("A Dignified Silence") on issues which society would prefer remain unvoiced and unquestioned. The *Radio* poems, with delightfully understated wit and humour, reflect the importance of the poet's relationship with language, communicating the understanding that in the realm of the poetic, as in the psychoanalytic, precision of language enables the articulation of something not heard before, that which normally resides outside of language, within the individual or societal unconscious or soul.

A sizeable number of the poems in this collection is gathered under the theme of Spain. Michael's love of and connection with Spain, particularly the region of Andalusia, form the basis of works detailing journeys and experiences at once physical, cultural, historical, emotional and spiritual. The various layerings in the poems describe a pilgrimage to territories of healing and belonging. The desire to become "A courageous son of Spain" expressed in "La Dama de Noche" evokes the spirit and work of Federica García Lorca, poet, playwright and son of Spain, whose work was inspired in large part by his native Andalusia. In their raw, sensuous descriptions of the landscape, history and culture of Andalusia as a realm which foregrounds aspects of life as "a dance with God a dance with Death" ("La Concha"), Michael's poems both express and embody *duende*. Described by Lorca as "the hidden spirit of our Spain of sorrows" which stretches across all barriers to reach the heart and the imagination, *duende* is the spirit possessing both art and artist, an essential element of authentic artistic production and performance, particularly within the indigenous Andalusian traditions' of the bullfight and of flamenco music and dance. Those traditions visceral expressivity, infused with *duende*, embody a proud and courageous affirmation of life in their confrontation with death, flamboyant and joyous in their expression of a spirit that death cannot silence. They have their exact poetic counterpart here in this collection. Those of us fortunate to have heard Michael use his voice to perform his poems have understood clearly the full meaning of Lorca's *duende*, and appreciate the bravura of *duende*'s artistic daring and grace when delivered by a master poet with an Irish accent.

While much of the work in this collection reflects the influences of Spain, it is important to underline that the poems remain grounded within an Irish literary tradition. In their expression of difficult truths often ignored or denied by contemporary societies, for example the pointlessness of life ("The Poppy"), or life's terror ("Seasons Change") and ambivalence ("Auburn"), the poems gather together traditional strands common to both countries. The concept of *duende* is echoed in Ireland's *sean-nós* song and dance tradition, where life, love and death form a thematic unity and where, as *sean-nós* singer and scholar Lillis

Ó Laoire describes, a concept similar to that of the Andalusian *duende* abides.

The quality of *dúil* (desire) infuses and emanates from the sean-*nós* singer, undergirding a song performance permeated by *brí* (life force, meaning) and *misneach* (courage), both essential qualities of authentic or "right" (*ceart*) performance which serves as a community celebration of life, often in defiance and subversion of societal restrictions. In both Spanish and Irish traditions as articulated in Michael's work, the dance with death is what imbues life with much of its passion and meaning. While the concepts reflected in these traditions are not easily translated into English, Michael has succeeded in creating that "new word yet to be spoken on earth" ("Nöeleen"). The meanings of those traditions are not readily accessible within modern/ postmodern culture intent on denying all that is associated with death, yet Michael captures the complex truth: "So changed from having lost/ Aware of limits lacking that much more/ I embrace the cost of a new life/ A second time around" ("The Daffodil"). With a deep understanding of such cultural elements, Michael's work leads a dance with language and with the poetic form that renders visible, audible and vital that which lives at the edges of language and of contemporary Western culture.

If that which is best in the poetic imagination is bound to express a vision that extols a freedom both personal and human, the *Sexuality* poems within this volume speak of and to the horror and "grotesquery" ("The People of the Book") of the historical and contemporary treatment of homosexuality by various regimes of power and authority, illustrating the diminishment of all sexuality inherent in such positions. "The People of the Book", establishing a dialogue between the voices of condemnation and the condemned, makes a powerful claim for the homosexual "dialect of sexuality" to be given place as part of the shared language both of humanity and of spirituality. The *Sexuality* poems and the *Love* poems forge a theology of belonging and inclusion, built on love and compassion and manifested in the ordinary life – between partners and lovers, between parents and children – sacred in all its humanity. The voice that reaches out in understanding and generosity in "To those who Have Given Up On Love" turns to celebration in "Epithalamion: A Poem for Terry", from which the collection takes its name. Written as a gift to Michael's partner, Terry, on the occasion of their Civil Partnership ceremony, the final poem in the collection gives voice to a simple, joyous celebration of love, which transcends the beloved, and celebrates the changes in Irish society that have enabled the public declaration and recognition of a dialect of love, hitherto condemned to a below-ground silence and invisibility.

The Irish poet Eavan Boland has described poetry as "a forceful engagement between a life and a language". As a manifestation of such a rich, honest and deeply moving encounter, the work in Michael Murphy's wisdom collection of twenty-five poems unearths and creates exchanges and dialogues between personal and universal journeys, navigating and mapping the human geographies of the mind, body, heart and spirit. The poems stand as an eloquent expression of the sacrament of the fully inhabited life, revealing its homeland as a region without borders to which all belong and are invited to return. *The Republic of Love* exhorts us to accept that invitation; as we are reminded in "Benedicite", "Yes is a sacred word".

Dr. Jeannine Woods,
School of Languages, Literatures and Cultures,
National University of Ireland, Galway, 2013.

A Chaplet of Roses Foreword by *Dr Jeannine Woods*

A CHAPLET OF ROSES IS a wreath of roses worn on the head, and also a rosary or string of beads used in counting prayers. It developed as a figurative sense from the original meaning of *rosarie*, or rose garden, conveying the idea of a "garden" of prayers. The poems in Michael Murphy's second collection of poetry are indeed beautifully contemplative. Each is a rose expressing love for his partner, for friends, for nature and animals and humankind. I also consider them to be true prayers, even though Michael writes "I feel bereft of God …" He continues in that particular poem, "Bereft", with an advanced interpretation of Christianity, emphasising a religious reality which is constructed out of language: "At least I have the language still/ To express impossible truths and capture the ineffable/ To underpin my life with meaningful myths/ The birth of immanence/ The crucifixion of truth/ The resurrection of hope/ And perhaps that final stage of growing up/ The ascension to mature human responsibility/ Without the joyful presence of my God/ With all the sharp-eyed clarity of a Presbyterian elder." All of the poems in this heartfelt collection continue this poet's exploration of a reality which is created out of language. They are informed by the three strands of Michael Murphy's career as broadcaster, psychoanalyst and author, and make for a deeply satisfying, rich and emotional engagement, featuring poems which reach out to touch the heart and appeal to the intellect.

There is an unremitting emphasis on the significance of love throughout this collection. In the poem "Enough", which he wrote for a friend who was dying, he concludes "Love was all that mattered/ In the end …" The opening poem, "And When You Speak of Trees" states that "… love is the firmest groundwork of our being / With roots to anchor truth …" In the poem "Bad Behaviour Can Get Elephants Killed", he says that "Animals do not belong to us/ They allow us to live near them/ To be graced by their honour/ To learn from their integrity/ To encourage gentleness/ And lay hold of tenderness/ To allow ourselves to love them/ And be loved a hundredfold in return …" And in the poem "I Shall Die", the poet first describes himself in humble terms, and then after having undergone the transfiguring power of love, he is repositioned: "I was an unimportant person … Nevertheless I was loved once/ By someone special/ And I loved him in return/ We glimpsed eternity together …"

For the first time, Michael employs his poetic gifts to examine his Irish heritage in a sequence of poems which speaks lovingly of his home in Castlebar, County Mayo. "Home To Mayo" is an anthem, the verses of which are designed to be sung or chanted in alternate parts. In this long and important poem, there is an unassuming line which captures the essence of this poet who feels misplaced, and gives us an explanation of the type of person we are dealing with: "In my mind I always live at home in Mayo …" He says, "I am the resurrection welling up/ From successive imprints on my soul/ They have written their names on my body/ Like the ancient ogham inscriptions on the standing stones/ Of Erris and Murrisk and Costello …" This linguistic imprinting on his soul and writing on his body from his Mayo ancestors have made Michael who he is. "My ancient roots are silently asleep/ Beneath the brown blanket bog of Ballycroy …" And he says, "Today it is my turn to give them voice/ To make known in my living all of their untold stories/ For the West is awake in me …" The centrality of place in imagining history, identity and community figures large in Irish tradition and in contemporary literature, notably in the poetry of Seamus Heaney and the dramatic works of Brian Friel. "Home to Mayo" builds on this tradition and on the theme of exile. There is longing in the lines "Mostly I miss the warm embrace of the Mayo accent/ That kiss on the lips blowing in off the Atlantic with the sea spray/ Soft and fierce and salty easy …" And he continues, "Mayo talk is a baptism that strengthens my spirit/ It fills me with hope and immerses me in certainty …" Three times he returns to the supplicatory refrain "These are my people/ This is my place" as if to underline and emphasise to those capable of hearing and understanding the necessity of that truth. In his work on language and landscape among the Western Apache, anthropologist Keith Basso points out that landscapes are not solely part of the material universe: "landscapes are always available to their seasoned inhabitants in other than material terms. Landscapes are available in symbolic terms as well, and so, chiefly through the manifold agencies of speech ... landscapes and the places that fill them become tools for the imagination ... eminently portable possessions to which individuals can maintain deep and abiding attachments, regardless of where they travel". The Mayo Sequence of poems illustrates the truth that those landscapes which we inhabit also inhabit us, and celebrates the imaginative possibilities of that co-(in)habitation.

The importance of the truth is a theme running throughout the collection, and is explained in "Home to Mayo" in terms of the poet's ancestry. Recalling 1798, and "those faithful Mayo patriots/ Who fought for their freedom at the Races of Castlebar/ First citizen President John Moore's republic/ Founded on being free to tell the whole truth without fear ...", he says, "We owe them the freedom to speak in the fullness of truth/ To let each Mayoman have his say without fear in this republic ..." Immediately he takes centre-stage in the poem by pointing out for the third time: "I am a Mayo man, born and bred/ I have the character of a Mayo native/ Who hails from the plain of the yew trees ..." with the strongest implication that he too be allowed to tell the whole truth, having previously explained in Mayo Irish: "If you traverse the talk on the *tóchar Phádraic*/ Avoid the *fóidín mearaí*/ Attend to the codes once hewn from a tree trunk of yew/ And be careful of the truth for fear of the oppressor/ I know the Mayo way ..." Again, the references to topographical features, place names and to folkloric beliefs reinforce the intimate connection between landscape, language, culture and identity, wherein place names and cultural readings of landscape may, as Basso points out, "be used to summon forth an enormous range of mental and emotional associations – associations of time and space, of history and events, of persons and social activities, of oneself and stages in one's life". In this Irish context, as the poem shows, such associations are most immediately accessible through indigenous, Irish-language names and terms. In conclusion, the poet co-inhabits Mayo's freedom-fighters, saying triumphantly: "They live forever like the yew tree when we attend to the truth/ When we value it voice it tell it and flaunt it like the red and green" (the Mayo colours).

The second poem in the sequence, "A Vote for Love", refers to the marriage equality vote, which has been incorporated into the Irish constitution. Michael says "I grew up gay in Castlebar/ Beyond the limits of language/ Displaced in the world without words ..." his alienation being due to a lack of speech. (In the poem "Hail and Farewell", the poet shows how the inability to speak – "I can never give that knowledge/ voice" – allows the truth to seep out in emotions more appropriate to other circumstances: "There is grief buried deep within/ Misplaced ... When I read out loud emotional poems/ Sorrow surfaces suddenly in the absent space/ Between the words"). The theme of language as a grounding principle, which surfaces in all the poems, gets full expression here. He says, "French literature delivered me salvation ... Saint Genet and Gide and Albert Camus ..." These are the writers who have influenced him, and he ruefully makes a joke against himself about his lack of sunny optimism "[They]Stole creative fire from the gods/ To illuminate my inner Mayo ..." which is a wry expression of the real hurt he suffered growing up gay at a time when homosexuality was illegal. I also enjoyed his witty relocation of the Greek myth of Sisyphus, with its Camusian echoes of the absurd: "Of imagining a solitary Sisyphus absurdly happy/ Climbing to the top of a cold Croagh Patrick ..."

As a broadcaster, Michael continually references in his poems the human voice as the ultimate means of salvation. For him, the human voice is the privileged medium of meaning. For the first time, the perspective has shifted onto the written word, which gets primacy here: "Book learning that privileged absence/ Reader and writer both invoking death/ Yet looking to speech as a present possibility ..." What Michael articulates is a clear reflection of the deconstruction philosophy of Jacques Derrida, again invoking salvation delivered by French literature. (Undecidable difference also surfaces in the concluding irony of the poem "Belfast": "And the eventual exodus of English gentry/ Leaving us the poorer for their absence/ And presence"). Michael says: "Pioneering writers wrote upon my soul/ They inscribed the vellum of my skin with sexual traces/ They founded me in a reality that fit/ They endowed me with a language of affirmation ..." And thus inscribed with Derrida's trace, he presents himself to us as poet by saying, "These words I wear have set me free ..." Of his origins favouring writing, Michael says, "My mother wrote yes to love ... She nourished me by writing yes for my lifetime ..." and, "My father wrote yes to me/ He underpinned my being with a covenant ..." "A Vote for Love" captures and reflects the extraordinary openheartedness seen during the campaign for marriage equality in Ireland, in which people of all ages and backgrounds came forward to voice deeply personal stories, experiences and hopes for themselves, their family members and their friends to be recognised as equal, and for that equality to be enshrined in the written text of the Irish Constitution: "The Mammies and the Daddies/ the Grandas and the Nanas/ Wrote yes: my child is cherished/ The same as any other". The poem concludes "The people of Ireland have voted yes for everyone/ They accepted into words what was not spoken ... Overturning years of hurtful judgements/ In the stroke of a pen ..." And there is relief in this conclusion, which also contains in the word "performance" a nodding reference to the tautological position of religion, which proscribes homosexual acts, even though being requires doing i.e. one cannot call oneself a poet without writing poems: "At long last recognition and performance/ For the limitless language of love ..." embracing gender equality. As he notices critically "Only silent churchmen barricaded dusty doors/ Against the greening breath of the Holy Spirit/ And the swelling surge of sexual truth ..." (In the poem "Complicity", Michael angrily returns to this theme of discrimination: "How do you condemn people who are gay/ But hold them in respect and with dignity/ When I hear such distinctions/ Bullying subtly with buts ... dare I name their rationalisation/ An opinion that was formed in advance/ Prejudice".)

Finally, in the third poem of the Mayo sequence, which lends its title to this volume, Michael comes to terms with the very recent death of his mother. This poem is hugely emotional, and uses the iconography of Mayo to describe his feelings during the funeral, from the moment of his mother's death to her burial. He has situated this poem at Old Head in Mayo, "Beneath the shadow of Croagh Patrick ..." The poet describes his mother's death in the contrasting terms of a soft, feminine sea, and hard, masculine land. The actual moment of her death is like a nuclear explosion, which changes the landscape: "Weighed down with giving/ I watched until you sank/ The blast hit before the absent surface calmed/ And then I turned and faced the land …" The poet has to face the future without his mother's presence, and in three brief but profound lines he enumerates what this means: "Stripped of a welcome/ No resting place left/ With nobody to tell …" He further draws on the folk-memory of the cruel clearances around Castlebar during the famine, to express his horror and terror at her death: "The crowbar brigade has brought death to a sound foundation/ A momentary fearful glimpse of what this clearance means …" His home is gone, and the foundation of his very being has been reduced to rubble. Succinctly, and very simply, he expresses the profound truth of such an irreplaceable loss: "I have lost someone/ who loved me/ Unconditionally …" He mourns the finality of her absence bitterly: "The tide on the turn shovelled up the sand/ And you were gone from me/ For ever …" (There are three lines in the poem "Devotion" which reverberate, and reflect light on the magnitude of the grief which Michael feels in relation to the loss of his mother. He says, "When I hold you to me in my arms/ I carry what is most valuable in all the world/ Access to your presence …" And in the poem "Hail and Farewell", he writes of what is unspeakable: "I kissed her goodbye/ And left/ I never saw her alive again/ I can never give that knowledge/ voice".)

Once again the poet describes in religious terms the transfiguring power of love, this time during the daily grind of mothering: "Your effigy infused an ordinary morning/ With all the rainbow colours of a mother's love/ In an extraordinary daily miracle …" After viewing his mother's body, Michael says, "I knew you were ordained a saint …" And he concludes the poem by referring to the apparition at Knock in Mayo in the context of mythological appearances of the goddess: "You came to me across the foam …" In a wonderful loving image of the mother and child, using gesture as speech, he delineates: "You didn't speak but held me in your gaze/ As once you cradled your first-born in the curve of an arm …" The last lines of this poem are not despairing, but draw together the strands of gratitude that permeate it. In the language of flowers, a chaplet of roses signifies beauty and virtue rewarded: "At my feet/ A chaplet of roses/ Floating gently on the ebb ..." And Michael makes a simple prayer to his mother in heaven: "Thank you/ For your legacy/ Of love".

The two poems about animals in this collection permit the poet a latitude in language. Michael uses the conceit to speak about women, and the misogynistic way they can be represented and spoken about. While telling the story of Tyke the elephant, who was shot by Hawaiian police after making a break for freedom, he writes: "The female died in a hail of gunfire/ Because she would not accept/ Being imprisoned in a circus/ Wearing ridiculous costumes/ Turning tricks for man's amusement/ For twenty years she suffered the insistent cruelty of clowns ..." The ironic implication in the title of the poem, "Bad Behaviour Can Get Elephants Killed", is that the female must remain under male control: "The public must be protected/ From a female on the rampage ... Because of her intelligence/ And her memory/ And the bigness of her heart". And he delivers the closing lines with the masculine certainty of a public news conference: "She had to be put down/ No question": the matter is closed; now, let's move on. In another poem which draws sustenance from the Billy Wilder film *Some Like It Hot*, Michael writes about a chocolate Labrador called Toga. Because he is referring to a dog, he is able to say things about the battle of the sexes in comedic language redolent of the Prohibition era: "And what do you make of her behaviour/ Coming in at two o'clock in the morning/ Some tramp from God knows where/ 'Honey, I forgot the time ...' Slut/ Charging down the hall/ And launching herself from the top step/ Onto Terry in the bed/ Licking him all over/ Slurp slurp slurp like her last drink in some cheap speakeasy/ You think a kiss will make this better?" The word "slut", meaning a slovenly or sexually promiscuous woman, is over six hundred years old. Though not used in polite, politically correct speech today, it is clear that Michael knows that the word "slut" also refers to a female dog, pointing to the historical denigration of women through their categorisation in derogatory, animalistic terms as a practice which endures in the present, even if the terminology has changed.

While writing an "Email to ISIS", Michael courageously posits the foreclosure of women, particularly by all religions, as the root cause of evil and insanity: "You blank them with burqas/ Negating their existence … They must have a male chaperone/ Otherwise you throw them off the highest building", demonstrating the true value they are accorded. He then asks a rhetorical question: "How could you be sane/ With your suppression of women/ Your refusal of the feminine side of your nature".

Through the labyrinth of language, Michael Murphy is sure-footed, although he recognises that language is problematic. The love poem "Devotion" manifests the instability of language. In the phrase "So thank you for choosing me/ To love/ To be intimate with", the apparent one-sided gratitude expressed for being chosen, which can be an unacceptable burden, is exploded in the next line, "to love". The verb refers to both the lover, but also to the person loved, who has been released through that choosing to love in return. Michael writes about the subject of language in the poem "The Seeker". As a poet, he says he is "… a seeker after truth/ Shooting arrows at a moving target/ Capturing truth with an onslaught of words/ Whose whittled tips sink home/ With the exploding poison of emotional recognition …" In the word "poison" the poet is recognising that the truth can be deadly, and also be open to dispute: curing or killing. As he says, his endeavour is "To create a language barrier/ Both protective and offensive/ A problematic personal reality/ Open to challenge and dispute/ Because you do not see me/ From the place where I see you …" Informed by his work as a psychoanalyst, Michael is speaking about the truth of subjectivity which is not a universal truth, but a particular one unique to each individual. He recognises that the truth is not a given fully formed, but is constructed in the dialectical movement between two people, meaningful only in the context of language: "I need you to help me/ Tell the truth/ Lacking your support/ I lie/ I speak false …" His conclusion is prayer, a pleading: "… let us be true to one another/ Striking the target/ Together".

In another poem, "Repetition", he refers to free-floating anxiety arising from "A linguistic net of language/ That catches insignificant gnats … Ties me up in knots" with the pun on "nots", indicating that his negation – the "inner Mayo" that he spoke about elsewhere – is due to fear. There is a phrase full of insight counteracting that anxiety in this poem, which bears fruitful meditation. Referring to the past, the poet realises "Yet everything that has happened/ Is the same: it just happened on different days ..."

In the poem "Seven", Michael captures the full meaning of the inability to speak, the absence of speech, through the story of Dermot, who witnessed the death of his friend when they were both seven years of age. It was a traumatic incident which left Dermot with a bad stammer. With empathic understanding the poet writes, "Later on when bullies mocked me/ Co-copied my st-stammer/ I stood there frozen unable to say/ Anything back quick-fire/ Some devastating put-down/ That began without a vowel/ Or a consonant just a hard scream/ So I thumped my attackers ..." Even though the poet is speaking about children, he is showing that the inability to speak leads to an acting out through physical violence. The words "frozen" and "thump" are a repeat. They recall the poet's earlier use of the words: "My friend frozen in the road/ I heard the thump the screaming brakes/ The pumping blood red/ When I was seven ..." which links the acting out to that devastating trauma. Throughout, Michael is using language that a child would use, frozen at that seven years of age.

Michael's joy in the use of language extends even into the local vernacular: "As I swaddle you with wealthy words from Cork ..." A glorious poem called "My Perfect Ruby" references a newborn through the alchemist's term for the elixir of life. It was written for his Cork friends on the occasion of the birth of their child, named Ruby, and he employs slang words from Cork to increase the sense of intimacy at this happy time, and uses the rhythmic lilt and phrasing of the Cork accent. "C'mere my perfect Ruby/ You took us by surprise girl/ When you landed here la/ Da berries – a welcome gift like – on-real/ Look at the gatch of you/ / Lying on your back with your doonchie arms in the air/ A bold Cork ball-hopper all balmed out ..." "Da berries" means the best happening; "the gatch" refers to the gait or personal deportment; "doonchie" means tiny; a "ball-hopper" refers to a mischievously humorous person; and "balmed out" is lying down, especially while sun-bathing, even in a mother's love.

In the poem "Bread", the poet uses conversational language to express the implied loneliness behind the breaking of bread at a meal: "Bread is such a shared pleasure/ The sheer goodness of it/ Don't waste it/ Eat up while you can/ There are people starving/ Did I thank you for inviting me?". Expatriates can feel isolated in the poet's beloved Spain, the location of this poem about sharing bread: "Have you had it with salt and olive oil …" In the poem "Figs and Blue Cheese", the poet contrasts the urban, impermanent holiday-land of sun umbrellas, with the rural, down-to-earth Spanish way they have always done things, through referring to "Figs and blue cheese/ Waiting on Wedgwood plates/ Under a white sun umbrella …" and "Salty cheese and succulent figs/ Overflow a cracked Cartuja plate/ Under an ancient olive tree …" He ends the poem on a surprising note: "A gift today for you and me/ To share with love and be inspired by". His use of the shimmering phrase "and be inspired by" is perfect in context, because for over seven hundred years "gift" has had the specialised meaning in English of "inspiration", which survives today in the word "gifted", meaning naturally talented. In the poem "Email to ISIS", Michael asks "Or will those few left alive …/ Be refugees fleeing the handiwork of a barbarian". The original meaning of "barbarian" referred to non-Christians, especially Muslims, which was gradually replaced by the meaning uncultured and ignorant, so that the poet's use of this particular word also references the underlying theme of the poem: "I see you have a passion for ignorance".

There is also a theme of valediction in many of the poems of this collection. In the tender poem "Enough", the poet writes, "Of that sundering moment of change/ When I shall fall through your loosening fingers/ Like water/ An exhalation towards the ultimate/ Setting me and our love story free forever/ To soar over an ocean of grief …" Michael expresses the brutal practicality of dealing with death in the poem "I Shall Die": "The pictures I collected the china I chose/ The book I was reading my toothbrush/ Stuff to be binned with the dead body in the bed". And he tackles the same subject of death in a humorous fashion in the poem "Interruption". Here he is writing once again on the subject of language: "I think I should sit down for death/ Such an ill-mannered interruption/ Deserves to be received seated/ To place a full stop in mid-sentence/ Is offensive and meaningless …" And the conclusion is delightfully ambiguous, where rudeness is happily entered into: "Nevertheless I shall sit down for Death/ As a personal protest/

To uphold a standard of behaviour/ Since I do know better/ Good manners should matter/ At least to me …" (Humour is also a theme running through these poems, notably in the poem "Kiwi": "The kiwi is such an unnecessary fruit/ About as useful as a decorative kumquat"). In the poem "Relationships Do Not Die", Michael uses a round to emphasise the continuation of life after death, in a further version of that imaginative "co-(in)habitation" about which I spoke earlier. The poem begins "Relationships do not die with death/ They live on in our bones". It concludes with the statement "They die only when I die". This apparent finality is immediately altered by a repetition of the glossing refrain "Relationships do not die with death/ they live on in our bones", meaning that those who survive him will carry forward the relationship in an unending cycle.

The poet boldly advocates rudeness as self-affirmation in the poem "On Turning Sixty-five", with his "… everything to do list …", which may take people aback, but there is hard-earned and healthy psychological wisdom in what this poet advocates: "Revolt and don't comply/ Become an annoying individual/ Drop people who aren't supportive/ Love the few/ Be truthfully rude to interfering relatives …" This is the advice with which viewers of his psychoanalytic-residency on the RTÉ afternoon television show will be familiar, and which holds out the promise of relief from carrying unnecessary burdens thrust upon us by the strictures of politeness or duty.

A Chaplet of Roses is a continuation of a journey begun in *The Republic of Love*, which navigates the territories of deep feeling and experience through the vehicle of language. If, as Michael has pointed out, language is a net in which it is possible to become tangled, the poems here demonstrate that it is also a web that weaves threads of connection between individuals and communities, expressing and underlining the interconnectedness of past, present and future, most especially through the enduring nature of love in its many manifestations. In its observations and explorations of themes which touch on many facets of human experience, Michael's poetry expresses truths at once deeply personal and universal in their resonances; it opens for the reader and listener a sense of place, at once unique and shared, which it invites us to occupy and cohabit along with our fellow travellers. His poems continue to flower in the heart and mind long after we close the pages of this beautiful book. In return, I quote the prayer of the poet's concluding words: "Thank you/ For your legacy/ Of love".

Dr Jeannine Woods
School of Languages, Literatures and Cultures,
National University of Ireland, Galway, 2015

The Ministry of Dreams Postface by Dr Jeannine Woods

THE MINISTRY OF DREAMS IS the third collection by the poet Michael Murphy. When Dr. Katherine Zappone was launching the psychoanalytic *Michael Murphy's Book of Dreams*, he introduced her as the Minister for Children and Youth Affairs. And she responded in her languid and educated American tones "Dearest Michael! If I may be so bold as to correct a distinguished author: I am the Minister of children who dream!" Michael wrote the concluding poem to honour her and her late partner Dr. Ann Louise Gilligan, whose pioneering struggle paved the way for marriage equality. A paraphrase of her remark gives the title to this extraordinary and affecting new collection of thirty-one poems.

The opening line is "Does my dog ponder the meaning of life..." All of the poems in the collection can be considered a guided meditation on modern Irish life. They nourish the soul at the same time as they appeal to the intellect with wit and compassion. These contemplations nudge the reader out of the comfort zone so that they can see life from another perspective. Always the music in these poems invites the reader and listener to draw their own conclusions: "The wider questions of desire evoke a slumping heartfelt sigh/ Like what is it all about really/ And whether the waiting around is worth it/ For those few circular moments of dancing excitement..." That question hovers over the collection, and here the mature truth does not trigger a threatened depression: "Her honey brown eyes give the game away/ And we collude in a reply by me tickling her under the ear/ While she licks my wrist in solidarity..." The redemptive value of connection through speech and gesture is the major theme of this whole collection. It is summed up in the clear-eyed but consoling final line of "My Dog and the Meaning of Life": "Does it get much better than this"

In his poem "On Writing", Michael refers to "...a need I have/

To speak myself/ To write myself/ To give myself away..." This collection is his most personal and revealing to date. It is raw at times. Michael gives himself away intimately in the Personal Poems section which is searingly autobiographical. The shattering poem "Polio and Getting Older" ends with the lines "I turned on the night light/ For when we need to visit the loo at two/ And again at four". People cannot but recognise that the comments in these poems have a universal relevance. In the poems he writes for his friends, or about his dog, his underlying philosophy of the transcendence of love shines through the different personalities: "To understand how love runs to catch us up/ And now accompanies us lightly every day/ Is a miraculous vision my dog has lived out in my presence/ So that I too have become a wonderful creature/ Loving and loved in her presence/ Truly human..." ("And I Am Truly Blessed"). In the poem he wrote for his friends Barbara and Tiernan we can hear the lines which again point towards redemption, where the "truly human" of the previous poem becomes "more like ourselves": "Seated around the table of your lives/ Breaking bread with wise friends companionably/ Nourishing our souls with sacred conversations/ That we can have with no one else/ That allow us to be more like ourselves..."

In the poem "A Life for Love", Michael refers to "...speaking myself/ *Mé féin a labhairt* .../ My being eddying along against the discursive current/ In a wondrous stream of words/ In spoken poems and the deepest ancient song..." The Irish phrase *mé féin a labhairt* loses strength in the deliberate English translation "speaking myself". He picks this up in "eddying along against the discursive current" which means attempting the impossible task of having to translate a whole Irish way of being into the English language, which is alien to the Irish spirit. The "spoken poems" also references the many shows he gave with colleagues around Ireland and in the Consulate General of Ireland and the Irish Arts Center in New York. The "deepest ancient song" is *cante jondo*, the most authentic form of Flamenco folk music from Michael's beloved Andalusia, and in Ireland it is *seannós*. This poem "A Life for Love" is an important disquisition on what it means to be an Irish poet giving himself away by putting his soul into English. Michael's description of Kris Kristofferson in "Joni Mitchell's 75th

Birthday Tribute" adds a further gloss on the truth of what is involved for the poet in speaking himself: "Realising this sudden intimacy was a very special moment/ A close-up view of an artist's open soul/ Singing his heart out and still prepared to bleed…"

The effort involved in writing so that the poet sings his heart out is costly on many levels, so it is enlightening to follow what Michael feels about writing. He says "The act of writing is so courageous/ Each word is a heartfelt journey into the unknown…" ("How I Could Help You"). His writing is not only an intellectual exercise in wisdom, but everywhere in this collection it is an evident matter of the heart. He expresses virtually the same sentiment in "On Writing", where the "heartfelt journey" becomes here "a triumph of the heart": "Wrestle doughty words onto the page/ For each one placed is a triumph of the heart/ And writing such a generous act of valour …" The word valour comes from the Latin to be strong, and strength is needed if you are to survive as a writer. "My partner asked me casually/ 'D'you think you might never get published again?'/ His question provoked terror …/ This must be what death feels like/ Unable to take another breath/ Oblivion …/ No words/ Ever". In the poem "Elysium", the poet avows 'I must swear truth/ Or be delivered speechless into Lethe's oblivion". There is another moment of very profound loss and alienation in speech, a sudden moment of penetrating insight, as the poet describes in "My Father's Language". Michael tells the story about attending a GAA match in Croke Park. Unlike his father he doesn't know how to behave, ostensibly because it was his first time there, and his county team Mayo lost: "With a crushing sense of being the loser/ I recognised the desolating truth/ That I'd never learned my father's language … And bereft of my father's version of reality/ I have no vernacular". How he has dealt with that social injury is evidenced in these wondrous poems which are redolent of his own unique voice.

Today valour means courage or bravery, especially in battle. And the full title of Michael's number one bestselling literary memoir is *At Five in the Afternoon – My Battle with Male Cancer*. The longest poem in this new collection delineates the reaction to the writing of his first book from some of his fellow townspeople. The title of the memoir was taken from a famous lament written by the Spanish poet Lorca, which

Michael mimics in a passage of this complex poem in order to increase its authority: "I wrote a book entitled At Five in the Afternoon/ The time the bullfighter battles the wild bull in the arena/ At five in the afternoon/ After the lament for his matador friend Sanchez Mejias/ At five in the afternoon ..." The poem is his own lament for a lack of understanding, and for what he terms in another poem "...the deplorables/ With their passion for ignorance..." ("Email to Donald Trump"). We are familiar with the Gospel quotation from Luke about "no prophet is accepted in his home town", and the word poet has been substituted for prophet here in the title of the poem "Poet in His Home Town". There is also a nod to Lorca's "Poet in New York".

In this collection, Michael has brought an extraordinary level of sophistication to bear on his ability to tell a short story through poetry. It is a major advance on his previous work. The apparent simplicity of the everyday language he employs – "There are occasional mornings/ When I am undone/ As I eat my cornflakes ..." ("Misericord"), or the poem about Terry's Mother Sarah "I spent my whole life thinking up/ New ways of cooking chicken" conceals a rigorous mind at work, most evident in this complex poem dealing with the theme of abuse in varying forms.

A man suffering from prostate cancer who believed he was going to die, who had to have his prostate removed in order to save his life, and who explained in the book that he had also suffered physical and sexual abuse, is assaulted again by people who should know better: "The book engendered a surprising reaction from some people in Mayo/ There were letters and phone calls from people I barely knew/ Telling me that what I described was untrue ..." In the phrase "people I barely knew" Michael is letting us know that in fact he does know those who attempted to undermine his reality. The poet is clear that he is not making a blanket condemnation of all Mayo people: just some. That word "some" reappears again further into the poem, highlighting how denial in this context is in itself a form of abuse: "If the protective psychological barrier that surrounds each one of us/ Has been breached by abuse in childhood/ Some people can sense the opening .../ They choose to enter in and have a go .../ Just because they can ... "In a statement that is shocking in its casualness, the poet is saying that people re-abuse the victim just because they can, and that it is a choice. Unfortunately, it is not unusual that the victim rather than the perpetrator is attacked when they break silence and tell the truth. This phenomenon has been all too pervasive in Ireland's destructive culture of silence and its treatment of abuse victims which continues into the present day.

The core section of the poem involves a dialogue between a neighbour and a Jesuit: "She told him my book was not well received in Castlebar/ Because it showed the town in a bad light/ The priest was astounded by this sleight of hand ..." because self-evidently the sympathy must go to the victim. When the Jesuit attempts to mollify the neighbour "Her response was a masterpiece of Mayo understatement/ Which covered a multitude/ "Well" she said "Michael always was/ A biteen different growing up... " This chillingly echoes the poem's later reference to the poet Lorca: "Shot by the vengeful hands of the Implacable Falange/ At five in the afternoon/ Because he was different".

The climax of the poem features an encounter in the Old Cemetery, which the poet uses as a framing device: "I want to go back to this poem's heritage/ In the Old Cemetery in Castlebar/ Johnny Mee was standing there talking .../ "Ah c'mere ould shtock, let me give you a hug ..."/ When I turned to go he called after me/ "I read your book Michael/ I read it/ Twice"/ He was letting me know that what I'd written/ Was fully understood by him ..." Johnny represents those who appreciate what Michael was trying to accomplish by his writing in adding to the collective corpus of truth. And the poet's conclusion is that "It was an immeasurably civilising moment/ For a poet in his home town ..." One might have expected him to use the words immensely civilised; instead he uses "immeasurably civilising", signifying the limitless and mutual redemption in this exchange, which forms a contrast with the one-sided and ignorant reaction of those who would prefer that truth be consigned to the shadows.

The complex way the poem is plotted with the various vignettes interlinking is masterly. For example, an incident that happens to his elderly mother when she was suffering from dementia is placed firmly within the section on abuse: "'Are you going on the lash tonight Sue'/ I saw my mother flinch at the language and shudder..." (Michael too has a reverence for language which was nurtured by his experience of newscasting, where every syllable had to be pronounced correctly).

Lest my practical criticism sounds like a psychological case history *pace* the psychoanalytic profession of the author – a critique which would fail to do justice to the breadth of Michael's work – I want to examine in detail the poetry in the final sequence of this poem. The poem ends with the poet's departure from his home town: "I drove slowly around the Mall/ Where once upon a time we played on the grass/ Within its protective linking chains and chestnut trees/ Past the house where I was born/ They've changed the colour on the hall door/ Heading straight for the road to Dublin/ Nothing left here to prove/ All gone/ It is time to move on" . The Mall is a circular green in the centre of Castlebar. That circular motif in driving around the Mall is a recurrence from the beginning when the grave is "surrounded" by yew trees, and also at the end where Michael is "surrounded" by his forebears. These circular references are broken by "Heading straight for the road to Dublin", echoing the earlier mention of the city as the homeplace of the loving chapter he wrote about Nöeleen Garber, "A Dublin woman living in Spain …" In other words, Dublin and Spain are linked in the poet's mind as places where loving people live. The Mall too was a haven: "Where once upon a time we played on the grass/ Within its protective linking chains …" Who is this "we"? The previous reference to chains in the poem refers to his dead brother Kieran, "Missing the absent link in the family chain". The idyllic nature of the brothers' childhood playing on the grass is gone forever when the protective chain is breached by death, or by abuse. The poet's journey has led him to the conclusion that there is "nothing left here to prove", meaning that at one time he did feel he had to establish validity, and he feels he has done that, paradoxically by handing the deep hurt done to him back to those with whom it originated. The refrain from the grave of his ancestors, "They are gone ", followed by the death of his brother, "Gone forever" culminates here in "All gone" – his ancestors, his playmate, his brother, his home, the town he grew up in and the people who knew him there have all gone. The outcome of the journey is the poet's realisation that "It is time to move on" and leave the "once upon a time" of the fairytale behind for good. The phrase he uses also indicates that new possibilities await in Dublin, or indeed in Spain.

Another singular short story brilliantly told in poetic form deals with adoption and belonging. It is deftly entitled "My Own Woman". Although horrifying, the poem is an enlightened portrait of a strong woman named Deirdre triumphing against the odds. We can read in the poem that Deirdre was rejected by her adoptive parents' relatives, and in later life rejected for a second time by her birth mother: "She did not remember my father/ Or which one of them I was". The pervading sadness in this poem gives the lie to those chocolate box presentations on television about finding relatives who grew up in different families, and everyone coming together and living happily ever after. The poet abhors such superficial relationships. There are a pithy two lines in this poem which make a very uncomfortable observation about attitudes in Ireland fifty years ago: "I fell pregnant and he went to the priesthood/ He left after a year and by then I was over in Dublin". As Michael goes on to demonstrate in the poem, a version of these prejudices is still alive today; witness the distancing comment about adoption from a bitchy woman in the golf club: "But not blood relatives Deirdre/ I know my husband couldn't do it". The central conceit in the poem is about an elephant, who never forgets. "From my own experience of being adopted/ And a growing up I cannot put aside/ People I can never forget or forgive/ I have been and will always be/ My own woman". Deirdre's conclusion is that she belongs to herself as a mature individual, and forgiveness is not the road for her.

Michael applauds using the shadow side of our nature to achieve maturity, for example in the poem "A Life for Love": "Which requires a more adult approach/ Than the human-lite notion/ That you have to love everyone/ Oh no you don't/ Love is very precious/ To be shared only with a chosen few/ Love is the highest value there is/ I choose to live a life for love/ Forgiveness". The penultimate line "a life for love" forces a new reading onto the last word e.g. for giveness, a giving he further explicates in the joyous poem Michael wrote on the birth of baby Matthew: "Giving offers one's hands and talents/ So that life can be easier… Giving makes a marriage gift/ To demonstrate belief in hope" ("His Royal Highness").

There are many love poems in this collection. In a poem written to his partner Terry called "Elysium", Michael says: "The good I did which brings forgiveness/ Which absolves me/ And makes me new/ Is that I have loved/ And been loved/ By you". The redemption that comes about through the mutual encounters previously seen in "Loving and loved in her service" ("And I Am Truly Blessed") or the meeting with Johnny Mee in the Castlebar cemetery ("Poet in his Home Town") is witnessed again in what the poet terms "a reciprocal act of love" ("Joni Mitchell's 75th Birthday Tribute"). The poet underlines the fact that speech always implies another person, and that conversation is ultimately a reciprocal act of love. In the poem "Full Speech", the poet draws inspiration from the artist Jean-Michel Basquiat. Having established "The human subject created through conversation ..." the poet goes on to make these statements about mature living: "Singing my own songs from the finished canvas/ In the consulting room/ Centre stage/ Living/ Of an analysis/ The end". The concluding moment in therapy is known as the end of an analysis. Michael inverts the words, so that he is also speaking about death at the end of our living, or a death in life through living without illusions. I also like the way this poem begins with a dry academic discourse: "Discourse is a unit of speech/ Used by university linguists for analysis ..." and goes through the psychoanalytic one: "The human subject/ Created through conversation/ With a personal psychoanalyst/ Who studies words and their placement/ Imbued with or soaked in my soul ..." to arrive at a place of artistic imagination where he could be describing his poetry: "In repurposed improvisations/ Chaotic collages that/ Anatomise the marginalised body/ Of the queer/ The outsider/ The local reject/ The truth".

In the poem "Loss", the poet anticipates the death of a partner, an occurrence which has a universal resonance: "Left remembering for an eternity/ the warmth of your body beside me/ In the cold loneliness of a double bed". Again in the concluding poem "I Am the Minister of Children who Dream" the poet paints a picture of the after-effects of a partner's death: "It is held in my heart as I start in anew/ Remembering that childhood truth of love/ Linking us forever like a necklace of threaded daisies/ Torn apart by death's withering hand/ The gathered petals painfully strewn across my heart for evermore ..." In the poem "Queen of the May" about the death of his aunt, Michael questions how life can continue after such a bereavement: "A beginning after a momentary pause/ Betraying the faithful truth/ Disastrously" i.e. the faithful and fateful truth of love is betrayed both by beginning again, and by taking just a momentary pause for the funeral. The poet's use of the word disastrously applies to an event that causes great distress, but it also implies that death is malevolent, literally ill-starred. This poem contains the foreboding lines "I cried in the car/ Unexpectedly/ Heading home/ Leading the retinue behind the coffin/ The next in line …"

Michael deals with ageing in this collection, and in a very personal and open way. The recognition in these wonderful poems involves and applies to everyone, whether dealing with ageing relatives, or with their own ageing. He issues an invitation to his partner: "Will you marry me at Michaelmas/ On the day the summer ends/ As the autumn is beginning…" And invoking Spain, the poet calls upon the metaphor of the brave matador: "Will you be bold with me and cheerful/ Play the hero one more time/ Vault the barrier to the arena/ Turn your back on getting older/ And trail your cape behind you/ Across the golden sands of time/ Acknowledging all supporters/ With a nonchalant wave of your hand" ("A Poem for Terry"). In the poem "Gaudete", the poet writes defiantly "I won't be overlooked/ Discarded or dismissed/ I'm determined to be taken into account/ For as long as I draw breath/ Not cast aside as useless/ Nor excluded just because/ I've lived a relatively long time/ Longevity is not a crime …"

One of the debilitating factors of ageing is increasing enfeeblement which the poet tackles head on in "Polio and Growing Older". Not getting older, but the more upbeat growing older according to the title. He paints a frightening portrait of the level of pain suffered by his partner. In the midst of anguish, there is an arresting moment of trust and real intimacy between the couple: "I'm in so much pain you would not believe"/ "Is there anything I can do to help?"/ "Would you mind opening my shoe laces/ And taking down my pants". In a startling reversal, prefigured by the opening two lines "My life partner suffers from polio/ As well as growing older with me" the poet inserts the following lines about himself: "Last year I could hunker down fish for the phone and spring back up/ This year I have to kneel on the floor and then haul myself up/ Leaning on the bed creaking quite a bit at the knees/ We're getting older/ I'm afraid …" The poet splits that rueful final phrase in two, which gives equal weight to both implications, and makes him apprehensive for the future. That apprehension is borne out in the love story written for and about Dr. Katherine Zappone and her late partner: "And I loved you then out loud and proudly/ Like a spinning top we soared towards the sun/ To the harmonic music of the spheres/ Until at dusk we all fall down to earth together". Dr. Zappone and her partner Dr. Ann Louise Gilligan published an autobiography entitled *Our Lives Out Loud – In Pursuit of Justice and Equality*. The children's nursery rhyme "Ring a Ring a Rosie" ends with the line "We all fall down" and suffer death.

There are moments of great humour in this collection. I loved the brothers' definition of a good woman: "The sign of a good woman" they proclaimed/ "Is one who can carry a bucket in either hand/ And open a gate with her knee" ("Brothers"). "A New Republic" is a devastating criticism of the social order: "How can you sleep easy in your bed/ While Irish men and women die in doorways/ While the banks foreclose/ And courts wage war against the poor" The poem begins with the lines "An Taoiseach Leo Varadkar says/ The rise in the homeless figures to ten thousand/ Is unbelievably frustrating/ Frustration is having to wait weeks/ for a table at Neven Maguire's …" irony nailing it and hammering it home. Or the apparently mundane exchange about criticism between Michael and Terry in "Polio And Growing Older", which turns into joy: "Is there a trousers ironed? I'll wear the light blue one tomorrow"/ "I didn't get a chance …"/ "You hear everything as a criticism my God/ They did a job on you in Castlebar/ And the fortune we spent on your therapy …"/ We laughed long and hard together". And also that wicked line "Priority boarding polio has its perks …"

There are *bon mots* of wisdom that pop up as you read these poems: the reference to Trump as "the Father of Lies" ("Madam President"); the observation "Christmas is a festival of memories" ("Christmas"); the concluding lines in "Joni Mitchell's 75th Birthday Tribute": "She kissed the side of his face/ He pulled her close in an embrace/ Then exited the stage abruptly/ Leaving her behind holding the microphone". That's what happened, but the old man was actually handing on the torch to a younger generation after exiting the stage. In "Eternally Yours": "We observed from afar/ That they were still seeing each other/ Noting the three-year engagement limit …". If he hasn't asked her to marry him after three years – next!

Michael pays tribute to the poets and writers who have influenced him. In "And We Shall Be A Blessing", he writes: "Led by the western fallen star/ Mourning the untimely death of the father/ His poet's soul listened to a little song of life/ Piping from within the sprigs of spring lilac/ Blooming perennially in the door-yard". The death of the protagonist's father is couched in the words of Walt Whitman's great lament on the death of Lincoln, the father of America. Whitman inaugurated the style of free verse which is Michael's preferred medium, and which he exercises in these poems so expertly. "Lorca With Whitman's Butterflies" pays homage to the greatest Spanish lyric poet Federico Garcia Lorca, who was taken out and shot at the beginning of the Civil War: "A last judgement on humanity/ Shot through with love/ Creating unspoken poems that softly bleed/ Gored by his hidden sexuality/ The deepest songs that have danced/ In slashes of male sweat to cicadas castanets/ Reaching for silence in a look/ Or in an elegant turn of the fingers/ Clawing at clay as he sinks/ In the face of unappeasable evil …" Michael makes use of the archetypal Spanish idioms of the bullfight and flamenco to express his horror at Lorca's murder, while recognising the poet's intrinsic homosexuality. On many levels Michael recognises the debt he owes to the Lorca: "We rise with the dawn in a suit of lights/ To speak powerfully in life's arena/ Imbued with the passionate grace of your poetry/ And we create our own universe/ Redeemed by your eternal spirit/ From the world of words that you have handled/ So that we see butterflies in your beard too/ Federico". The butterflies reference is to a line from one of Lorca's most important poems, "Poet in New York". The slang word for homosexual in Spanish is *mariposa* or butterfly. The power of literature and love to bequeath lasting legacies is also highlighted in "A Life for Love", which closes with the beautiful image of French writer and philosopher Michel de Montaigne: "And maybe Montaigne really meant/ Death to find him planting love/ Instead of his cabbages/ Indifferent to doing and having and seeming/ Singing his last song happily/ Simply being".

Finally, for anyone who has visited Ground Zero in New York, I must make mention of the poet's superb description of the 9/11 memorial, which becomes in his understanding a comment on the state of our world: "At Ground Zero where the water washed souls clean/ Falling down forever/ the overflow of horror inundating the abyss/ I saw the water disappear into the black hole of our existence/ Oh so lonely/ The deafening sound of civilization drowning…" ("Brothers").

I feel grateful for being able to read the beautiful words in this collection. I did not say beautiful poems because the sentiments expressed in some of them are deliberately ugly, and deal with the shadow side of life. Those few serve to place the many others into a higher relief. And both together encompass the truth. As the poet says so eloquently about bringing balance into your life: "Play at the centre of the see-saw/ Only occasionally come down hard at one end/ And soar towards the sun from the other/ Those singular moments to make you feel immortal/ Before you sink again into the ordinary's embrace …" ("The Madrid Journalist"). All of the poems in this collection uplift and grant courage to continue living life in hope, both in the light as well as in the shadows: "I have to be able to freely choose/ To live untied an inalienable life/ To win the struggle striving/ And contend while losing continually" ("Heretic"). The freedom that is described in these poems is inspiring. It kindles the wish to be a better human being, as the poet continues to guide a gentle but revolutionary way forward: "Freedom from the tight pull of constraint/ And the handing down of deadening custom/ Allowing the greatest possible freedom to determine selfhood/ The freedom to realise one's own temperament fully/ The freedom for absolute self-affirmation/ Of all that constitutes the individual human being …" ("And We Shall Be A Blessing").

If I may be so bold to end these comments by quoting the distinguished poet against himself, and to offer his own words back to him to express our gratitude for having sung his heart out in our presence, being prepared to bleed. My reaction is that these shining poems have added to the sum of goodness in our world: "We feel grateful for the richness/ You weave into the weft of our existence/ A wealth of love and laughter/ Contributes texture to the matter of our lives/ Bearing witness to each other adds a purpose to our quest ..." ("Love that is Always Here"). It is my privilege to commend to the poet's readers and listeners all of the poems in this extraordinary and heartfelt collection.

Dr Jeannine Woods
School of Languages, Literatures and Cultures,
National University of Ireland, Galway, 2019

Acknowledgements

These are the people who support and promote my writing, and I offer each of them my heartfelt thanks:

Ciana Campbell, presenter and broadcaster.
Fiona Coffey, literary agent and publicist.
Robert Doran, copy editor and proofreader.
Colin Eaton, artist, architect and artisan.
Andrew Brown, cover designer.
Anne Kearney, digital promotion.
Chenile Keogh, production director, Kazoo Publishing.
Margaret Martin, tour manager and researcher.
Terry O'Sullivan, life partner and sounding board.
Anna Timmermann, creator of an inspiring writer's environment in Spain.
Jeannine Woods, National University of Ireland, Galway.
My friends and former RTÉ colleagues, Eileen Dunne, Eamonn Lawlor, Emer O'Kelly and Deirdre Purcell, who presented a selection of these poems at venues all over Ireland and in the United States.